MINDFUL ME!

GAURANGA DARSHAN DAS

ILLUSTRATIONS
CHARBAK DIPTA

SCHOLASTIC
New York Toronto London Auckland
Sydney New Delhi Hong Kong

Published by Scholastic India Pvt. Ltd.
A subsidiary of Scholastic Inc., New York, 10012 (USA).
Publishers since 1920, with international operations in Canada,
Australia, New Zealand, the United Kingdom, India, and Hong Kong.

For information regarding permission, write to:
Scholastic India Pvt. Ltd.
A-27, Ground Floor, Sigma Centre
Infocity-1, Sector 34, Gurgaon-122001 (India)

First edition: May 2024

ISBN-13: 978-93-5954-162-4

Printed in India at Polykam Offset New Delhi 110028

Every child is a story yet to be told,
a dream waiting to unfold.
Groom them with Gita wisdom and
watch them grow to their full potential.

Praise for the Book

This book reflects Gauranga's experiences [...] making his advice not only relevant but also relatable. *Mindful Me!* is a well-equipped toolbox helping young minds navigate life's challenges and dealing with them with a sense of calm and mindfulness in tandem with ancient texts. I hope this book reaches children and helps them become more mindful.

—Sachinandan Swami (Educator and Senior Monk, ISKCON)

Mindful Me! [...] offers a beautiful gift to the modern child to become mindful and stress less. Through skillful integration, the author creates a rich tapestry of guidance, empowering young readers to navigate life's challenges with clarity and courage.

—Dr Vijay Bhatkar (Scientist, Educator, and IT Leader)

Mindful Me! [...] is a transformative guide inspired by the timeless wisdom of the Bhagavad Gita, tailored specifically for children. This is not just a book; it's a companion for every child seeking inner peace, confidence, and joy amidst life's ups and downs.

—Dr Shubha Vilas (Author, Educationalist, and Leadership Consultant)

This book is a beautiful gift for kids, enabling them to rise above the chatter of their minds. *Mindful Me!* will lead them to a path of wisdom [...] steering their lives towards achieving lasting mindfulness.

—Shriya Saran (Actor and Dancer)

Mindful Me! serves as an intriguing and inspiring masterpiece for today's children to introspect and cultivate mindfulness.

—Neeraj Choksi (Business Leader)

Contents

Author's Note

In our fast-paced modern world, stress, distress and distraction have become all too common, affecting people of all ages, including children. People from all walks of life are on a quest for effective strategies to manage these challenges and cultivate resilience and concentration. And one way to achieve this is to become mindful!

Welcome to *Mindful Me!*—a kid-friendly journey into the realm of concentration, de-stress and fulfilment, primarily based on the teachings of the Bhagavad Gita and similar such timeless wisdom texts. The Bhagavad Gita is a great wisdom song sung by the Almighty God Krishna to motivate his depressed friend, Arjuna. The Gita cleared the confusions in Arjuna's mind and brought clarity in his thoughts. Similarly, Gita's wisdom can take us on a journey from confusion to clarity, distraction to concentration, and distress to de-stress.

The Gita is like a life manual that presents several lessons and actionable tips to lead a meaningful life. It teaches us the art of mindful living, navigating life's challenges with determination, spiritual intelligence and inner strength. The universal message of the Gita is relevant for all age groups and individuals of different backgrounds.

Mindful Me! provides simplified explanations, relatable examples, interesting anecdotes, engaging exercises and practical tips to assist children in effectively handling stress and adversity, and provides tips to practise mindfulness. The book's approach is holistic, addressing various facets of life, including personal, academic and emotional well-being, making the learning process not only effective but also enjoyable.

Within these pages, you'll explore the causes and symptoms of stress and distress in kids, as well as practical tips to alleviate them. The profound topics of this book are presented in a child-friendly and light-hearted manner, accompanied by stories and interactive exercises that children will find not only helpful but also relatable. This book empowers kids with cool tools to take charge of their stress, become mindful, and navigate life's challenges with confidence and courage.

While the primary audience for this book is kids, it extends its benefits to anyone interested in enhancing their mental emotional, and physical well-being. So, let's embark on this journey together and learn how to be mindful, stress less, and live more!

– Gauranga Darshan Das

From DISTRESS to DE-STRESS

SECTION 1

Childhood is a happy phase of life where there is innocence, adventure, boundless energy, and unbridled enthusiasm. It's a memorable time for every kid and their parents. However, even these young minds, so full of potential and promise, may have to face the brunt of stress at times.

This section of the book describes various causes and symptoms of stress in kids. They are not to be underestimated; they are significant guideposts indicating the need for support and guidance. Here, you'll also find several tools to address the stressors for your overall emotional well-being.

By recognizing, acknowledging, and taking guidance in managing your stress, you will be empowered to become resilient, confident, and mature and grow as wonderful individuals who can face life's challenges with courage. This way, you can ensure a mindful and merry childhood with a bright and promising future.

1 Positive and Negative Stress

Hanuman Sketch and the Rubber Band

It was 4 p.m., and nine-year-old Arav had just returned from school. Excitedly, he declared to his mother, 'Mom, my teacher gave me an assignment to draw Hanuman.'

'Great! Take some rest and then get started,' his mother replied.

Arav proceeded to take a bath, enjoy some snacks, and retreated to his room, closing the door behind him. At around 8 p.m., he emerged with a broad smile.

'Mom, I spent three hours making this sketch of Hanuman. It was very tough, and I had to make multiple attempts, but finally, it took this wonderful shape!'

Arav's mother smiled warmly as she looked at his beautiful drawing, appreciating the efforts he had put in. 'That's great, Arav! I'm proud of your hard work. You see, sometimes challenges can bring out our best talents. I understand it was a bit stressful for you initially, but it was positive stress that brought out the best in you.'

'Yes, Mom! How should I take it to school? It's too big to fold.'

'Well, place this butter paper on top of your sketch and roll it up carefully. I will give you a rubber band to hold it together.'

Arav followed his mother's instructions, but he found the rubber band too small to bind his drawing roll. Then his mother demonstrated how to stretch the rubber band gently and fit it around the rolled-up drawing.

Arav, then, eagerly gathered some extra sheets and tucked them along his Hanuman sketch. However, the rubber band broke as it couldn't bind so many sheets. Arav turned to his mother for help.

'Arav, remember, the rubber band has elasticity. It is stretchable but has its limits. If you stretch it beyond its limits, it will break.' She then took a larger rubber band and secured all the sheets.

She continued, 'Arav, just like the rubber band, we can also stretch ourselves to grow and learn but we must be careful not to overdo it. Overstretching, whether it's a rubber band or our minds, only leads to breakdown. Some positive stress is required for us to reach our full potential, just as you worked hard for three hours to create this beautiful Hanuman sketch. But staying up all night to complete it would have been detrimental to your health, right? So, we need to understand how much is too much.'

Arav's mother comforted him and calmly shared the life lessons they learnt from the rubber band.

Takeaways from the Tale

- Hard work and persistence yields success.
- Challenges uncover hidden talents.
- Positive stress helps us reach our inner potential.
- Know your limits and don't overstretch yourself.
- Strike a balance between effort and health.

Types of Stress

Stress is a common aspect of life. Everyone experiences it. But sometimes, we may not fully understand what someone means when they say, 'I am stressed!' The word 'stress' can have various meanings based on the context in which it is used. Prominently, there are three types of stress.

1. **Physical stress** is the discomfort that we feel in our bodies, such as body aches and headaches.
2. **Verbal stress** is a form of speech that places extra emphasis on a specific point, making it stand out in the conversation.
3. **Mental stress** is a state of emotional strain or tension that arises when we face challenging situations. This kind of stress is a natural reaction to potential difficulties and can affect how we feel when dealing with difficult circumstances.

We experience these types of stress in our day-to-day life. In this book, we will discuss mental stress, simply called as 'stress'.

Stress is how your mind reacts to something that feels tricky or a bit tough. It can happen when you have an important test at school, a game, or when you're worried about other things.

The Balance of a Bowman

Imagine a bowman who wants to shoot an arrow at a target. He places the arrow on the bow, pulls back the string with the arrow, and then lets it go. If he doesn't pull the string back enough, the arrow won't go with the desired force and speed. On the other hand, if he pulls the string too hard, he might even break the bow. So, he needs to find the right balance to make the arrow fly.

This is similar to how stress works in our lives. To make progress in our life and grow maturely, we need some challenges and tough situations. These are like the workouts for our minds and hearts, just like exercise helps our bodies become strong and fit. But if we have too much stress, it can cause problems.

How much stress is too much? Well, it really depends on the person and the situation. It's like finding that right balance, just like the bowman finding the right pull on his bowstring to hit the target.

Depending on the intensity of stress and its effects on a person's mind and body, mental stress can be classified into two distinct categories:

1. Positive Stress
2. Negative Stress or Distress

Positive Stress

Positive stress is when the stress is just right, not too much and not too little. It's like a little push that helps you work hard and do your best. This kind of stress is good because it motivates and energizes you to grow up to your full potential.

For example, when you're getting ready for an important school presentation, the stress you feel can make you do your best. And think about the excitement of planning your birthday party—that's a bit of stress, too, but it's a fun kind! You feel really happy when you work hard and do well in such situations.

Positive Stress Fosters Focus: Sometimes, if we give ourselves too much time to do a small activity, we end up wasting a lot of time. But if we set a reasonable deadline for ourselves or accept a deadline set by our parents or teachers, it helps us become more focused and determined in our work. This can save us from unnecessary distractions and improve our productivity.

Time-bound work with a target, under a reasonable amount of stress or pressure, can bring out the best in us. It can make us more organized and prevent us from wasting time.

While positive stress fosters focus and determination, negative stress can create complex situations.

Negative Stress

Negative stress, on the other hand, is when stress becomes too much to handle. Stress that crosses tolerable limits takes a shape of suffering and discomfort. It is often associated with emotional pain and can have detrimental effects on an individual's well-being.

It can make you feel overwhelmed, like you can't cope, or it might make you feel sad, upset, worried, and scared. It can even cause problems for your body and mind. Such negative stress actually causes distress.

Distress can come from big problems, like when someone you care about is very sick or when you're having a really hard time at school. When you're feeling distressed, it can be hard to be happy or feel well. It's important to get help and find ways to feel better when you have distress.

Stress that turns into distress can manifest as symptoms of anxiety, depression, physical health issues, lack of concentration and a reduced ability to function effectively.

Dealing with stress begins by identifying the causes of stress. The first approach in identification is observation and introspection. Further, one can consult parents, siblings, and reliable friends to detect the reasons, based on their observation.

The following are a few causes and symptoms of negative stress. There can be many more depending on the individual.

Causes of Stress

- Academic Pressure
- Extracurricular Activities
- Parental Expectations
- Peer Pressure
- Bullying
- Social Anxiety
- Sibling Rivalry
- Family Issues
- Lack of Sleep
- Social Media Exposure

Symptoms of Stress

- Mood Swings
- Withdrawal
- Irritability
- Poor Concentration
- Sleep Disorders
- Irregular Eating
- Physical Symptoms
- Strange Mannerisms
- Regression
- Isolation

The list of the causes and the resultant symptoms of stress can be as expansive as the sky, but one can considerably avoid these causes and the symptoms by following some practical and effective tools given in the remainder of this section.

The relationship between causes and symptoms of stress can be complex and you may exhibit a combination of these symptoms in response to various stressors. For instance, academic pressures can lead to poor concentration, peer pressure can lead to erratic behaviour, bullying can lead to isolation, family issues can lead to mood swings, excessive media usage can diminish social interactions, and inadequate sleep can decrease productivity.

TRY THIS OUT!

Analyse your own mind and identify the causes of your stress and the resultant symptoms.

Balancing Positive and Negative Stress

Positive stress is beneficial but negative stress can be harmful. However, a complete absence of stress can lead to complacency, laziness, and underperformance, which we should avoid.

In the aforementioned story, Arav experienced some stress to complete his assignment of making a sketch. However, this was a positive stress that helped him discover the wonderful artist within himself and enabled him to create a beautiful sketch in a short span of time. At the end of this challenge, he felt alive, energized, and encouraged. Also, he learnt beautiful lessons from his mother through understanding the concept of a rubber band. What can we learn from this? Here are some crisp, actionable tips for you from Arav's story.

- **Welcome Challenges:** Assignments and challenges are like exciting adventures where you get to show your creativity and skills. They can help bring out the best in you. Don't shy away from them otherwise you might not be able to discover your true potential. Embrace positive stress courageously. So, get onto it instead of getting away!

- **The Fruit of Hard Work:** Putting effort into your tasks, even if it feels challenging or stressful, can help you discover your talents and achieve amazing things. Devoting three hours to complete a Hanuman sketch right after school isn't really a piece of cake. But the result of all that hard work was tastier than a piece of cake. So, let's nurture the hard work tree and relish the fruit it bears.
- **Avoid Laziness:** Until Arav didn't stretch the rubber band to its full capacity, he couldn't accommodate all his sheets within it. Similarly, when we don't step out of our comfort zones due to laziness and complacency, we won't be able to achieve our goals, despite being fully capable. We need to give up lethargy to discover our abilities. Keep learning and improving, little by little.
- **Don't Overstretch:** When Arav stretched the rubber band beyond its limits, it broke. While it's good to push yourself to grow, we should know how much is too much. When we overstretch ourselves by being overly passionate and overly ambitious about results, we may experience breakdowns, just like the rubber band. A little further and the rubber band would

have been reduced to a piece of useless rubber. Similarly, identifying and drawing out our limitations while working to the best of our ability will make sure that we don't snap up like an overstretched rubber band!

- **Learn from Mistakes:** We can't always do things in the right manner. No human being is completely perfect in everything. Making mistakes is normal and there is no need to feel discouraged, disappointed, or disheartened. We grow and improve when we learn from our missteps.
- **Learn to Balance:** Positive stress can motivate you but too much of it can be harmful. It's essential to find the right balance, just like Arav did with the rubber band. Striking the right balance between pursuing your goals and taking care of yourself is necessary to lead a happy and successful life. We must accept stress only to the extent that it boosts our productivity. Otherwise, we may end up weary and burdened.
- **Seek Guidance:** The right balance varies for each individual, therefore, we should reflect on our efforts and seek guidance from parents, teachers and experienced well-wishers to understand how much stress we need to excel in whatever we do. They can guide us when we are confused or stuck in a tricky situation just as Arav's mother helped him.

The Art of Tolerance

Everyone feels stressed sometimes, and that's normal! But it's important to manage it before it becomes overwhelming and turns into distress. Anything that crosses limits causes problems—whether it be overstretching, overstressing, overeating, oversleeping, overtalking, and so on. Talking to parents, teachers, or friends can be a helpful way to cope with stress when things feel too difficult.

Sometimes, the only way to deal with stress is to develop the ability to tolerate it. It's not always possible to find a solution for every problem, but time heals everything. Knowing the temporary nature of happy and distressful moments, we need to learn not to get overwhelmed by such experiences, as Lord Krishna teaches us in the following shloka:

Thus, tolerating the trivial situations of life is like a superpower that can help you grow through life's adversities!

Now that you know what positive and negative stress is, let's explore how to deal with various causes of negative stress like academic stress and peer pressure in the upcoming chapters.

mātrā-sparśās tu kaunteya
śītoṣhṇa-sukha-duḥkha-dāḥ
āgamāpāyino 'nityās
tāms-titikṣasva bhārata

The contact between the senses and the sense objects leads to happiness and distress. But these experiences are temporary. They come and go like the winter and summer seasons. One must try to tolerate the temptations caused by the senses and mind without being disturbed.

(Bhagavad Gita 2.14)

TRY THIS OUT!

Identify some day-to-day activities in your routine where there is a possibility of overdoing things and leading you into trouble.

HELP OTHERS

Engaging in volunteer activities is a fulfilling way to make a positive impact on others and yourself. It provides a sense of purpose and accomplishment, countering negative stress with the joy of contributing to the community. Serving others fosters connections, builds community, and creates a positive ripple effect that extends beyond immediate benefits. So, let's have fun and make this world awesome through service!

2 Academic Stress? Try TAP Management

Stones of Success

Ajay, a bright student, had just entered the seventh grade. Although he was good at studies, he found himself drowning in a sea of assignments, homework, and exams.

The transition to a higher grade had proven more challenging than he expected. With a heavier workload and even more demanding subjects in tow, Ajay struggled to manage his time effectively. Every night, he found himself buried under a mountain of textbooks, notebooks, and unfinished assignments. The stress of looming deadlines began to take a toll on his enthusiasm for learning.

One day, Ajay's elder sister, Aruna, a college student majoring in psychology, noticed the visible signs of stress on her brother's face. Understanding that her brother needed more than just sympathy, Aruna decided to share some of the organizational and time management skills she had picked up during her college years. She explained to him the importance of setting priorities, breaking down tasks into manageable chunks, and creating a realistic schedule.

'Consider your time as a limited jar with tasks as stones—larger tasks being the bigger stones, and smaller tasks represented by pebbles,' Aruna wisely advised.

'Now, if you start by putting the smaller pebbles into the jar first, there won't be enough space left for the larger stones, which represent more important tasks. However, if you start by placing the larger stones, representing more important tasks, you'll ensure that the crucial aspects of your day are addressed. Once these major tasks are in place, you can then add the smaller stones, symbolizing smaller tasks. The smaller tasks will fill in the gaps, allowing you to efficiently complete both the essential and low-priority aspects of your work. This strategic approach enables you to manage your time effectively and accomplish your entire workload in a more organized and satisfactory manner.'

Together, Ajay and Aruna identified the subjects and assignments that required immediate attention. Aruna helped Ajay create a daily and weekly schedule that included dedicated study time for each subject. She emphasized the significance of taking short breaks to avoid burnout and encouraged him to communicate with his teachers about any challenges he faced.

As the days passed, Ajay began to notice a positive change. The chaos of scattered assignments and unorganized study sessions transformed into a structured routine. With Aruna's guidance, he learnt to prioritize tasks, manage his time efficiently, and approach his studies with a more focused mindset. He wasn't stressful like before.

Aruna's support extended beyond mere academic guidance, she became a pillar of encouragement for him. Whenever he felt overwhelmed, Aruna was there to remind him of his capabilities and offer a helping hand.

By the end of the semester, Ajay not only managed to flourish academically, but also discovered a newfound confidence in his ability to handle challenges. As they celebrated his improved grades and sense of accomplishment, Aruna smiled at her brother and said, 'Remember, Ajay, you're capable of so much more than you think. All it takes is a little sense of organization and the belief that you can do it.'

With his sister's guidance, Ajay learned valuable life skills that extended far beyond the realm of academics. Through their shared journey, they proved that sometimes, all it takes is a helping hand and a bit of structure to turn overwhelming chaos into a manageable path to success.

Takeaways from the Tale

- Organize your priorities, like stones in a jar.
- Divide overwhelming tasks into manageable chunks.
- Create a structured routine to ensure effective study sessions.
- Avoid burnout by incorporating short breaks.
- Openly communicate with elders and seek guidance.
- Be organized and believe in your abilities.

TAP: Time, Attention, and Priority Management

Sometimes, the tasks at school might seem like there's not enough time to fit them all in. It's like having a jigsaw puzzle with a thousand pieces and you're not sure where to start. But effective self-management can do it all for you.

As a student, you can easily expect that sometimes schoolwork can be overwhelming with many tests, projects, and activities. If you are mentally prepared, you will not be too shocked or stressed when the busy time arrives.

Here's a special strategy that can help you cruise through all your tasks at school in an efficient and stress-free way. For easy recall, we call it 'TAP' Management. TAP implies Time, Attention, and Priority:

- **Time Management:** Everyone, from kings to soldiers, CEOs to employees, high achievers to struggling students, shares the commonality of having only twenty-four hours in a day. The key to success without undue stress lies in the effective management of this limited resource. Embark on the journey of categorizing your tasks into the less important and more important and witness how efficiently adjusting your time transforms time management into a seamless endeavour!
- **Attention Management:** Your energy levels and attention levels can vary throughout the day, with times of high activity and moments of fatigue. Utilize your peak periods to tackle the most critical tasks and reserve your not-so-active times for others.
- **Priority Management:** You may have a multitude of tasks, but you need to differentiate between the critical ones from the minor ones. Some tasks are naturally more important than others. Learn to prioritize the most crucial ones.

Five-Step Plan to Deal with Academic Stress

TAP management is like having a treasure map. It helps you plan your time wisely so that you can complete your work without feeling rushed, stressed, or overwhelmed. Here's how you can do it:

Step 1: List your tasks: Write down all the tasks you need to do during the day, week or month. Note them down, regardless of whether they are big or small.

Step 2: Categorize the tasks: Categorize tasks based on their nature and size. Some tasks require creativity while others may be simple or mechanical. Certain tasks demand more time or a higher level of focus, while others can be completed quickly and easily, even on the go.

Step 3: Set priorities: Start with the major and most crucial tasks first. Once you finish those, you can move on to the minor ones.

Step 4: Break tasks into smaller pieces: Break big tasks into smaller, manageable pieces. Then set targets or deadlines for completing the smaller ones.

Step 5: Create a schedule: Make a daily or weekly schedule. You can use a colourful calendar with stickers or drawings to make it interesting. Mark and mention the time when you have to do your homework, study for tests as well as conduct other activities.

Step 1	**Step 2**	**Step 3**	**Step 4**	**Step 5**
List your tasks	Categorize the tasks	Set priorities	Break tasks into smaller pieces	Create a schedule

Imagine your schoolwork is a treasure hunt. Your schedule is like the map that shows where the treasures (completed assignments) are hidden. By following the map, you can find each treasure one by one. For instance, if you have a big project, breaking it into smaller steps is like solving riddles to find the ultimate treasure. Use a colourful calendar to keep track of your assignments and tests. In this way, you can manage your time wisely and complete your school tasks without feeling stressed.

Right Things at the Right Time

Lord Krishna states the following on time management in the Bhagavad Gita:

yā niśā sarva-bhūtānāṁ
tasyāṁ jāgarti saṁyamī
yasyāṁ jāgrati bhūtāni
sā niśā paśyato muneḥ

What is night for everyone is the
time of awakening for the wise; and the time of awakening
for everyone else is night for the wise.

Bhagavad Gita (2.69)

In various wisdom texts, including the Bhagavad Gita, it is emphasized that individuals are influenced by the three gunas (modes of nature)—*sattva*, *rajas,* and *tamas*—which are also associated with different times of the day.

According to ancient wisdom, human behaviour is intricately linked to these three gunas. These are not only philosophical concepts but also relate to different times of the day. In the early morning, *sattva*, which represents goodness and purity, prevails. The afternoon is associated with *rajas*, signifying passion and activity, while the night is dominated by *tamas*, representing ignorance and inertia.

The Bhagavad Gita and many other profound texts suggest that aligning our activities with these natural rhythms can enhance our productivity and overall well-being. It is recommended to harness the *sattva* of the early morning by engaging in spiritual practices, meditation and acts of devotion, which can set a positive tone for the day. The *rajas* of the afternoon is an ideal time for action-oriented tasks and productivity. Finally, the *tamas* of the night is a time for rest and rejuvenation, which is crucial for maintaining a healthy balance.

Incorporating these principles into our daily routine, such as rising early for meditation and spiritual activities, can help optimize our productivity, resulting in a more balanced and fulfilled life.

If we want to achieve concentration and focus in completing our academic tasks, it is best to finish them during the early hours of the day. Postponing work to do it later in the day can lead to greater difficulty as our minds and bodies tire with the day's progression.

Time management is like a secret tool to make school less stressful. When you plan your time well, you can find the right balance between your schoolwork and free time that can be used to relax and play.

While academic stress can be handled by TAP management, there are other sources of stress for growing kids, such as stress from comparison. Check out the next chapter for some cool tools to deal with this devil of comparison.

TRY THIS OUT!

Organize your upcoming week by employing the TAP management framework. Categorize and prioritize all your activities and tasks according to the schedule that you've crafted. As the week unfolds, observe the remarkable efficiency with which you accomplish your work. Then revel in the satisfaction of having executed your plans with precision and ease by the end of the week—a happy celebration of your accomplishments!

3 Tired of Comparisons?

Race or Quest?

Once upon a time, in a classroom, a math teacher asked a student, 'What if you get 60 per cent in your exam? Would you be happy?'

A student replied, 'Not really. It's not a great score.'

The teacher continued, 'What if one of your friends gets 50 per cent, another 40 per cent, and the other gets less than that?'

The child thought for a moment and said, 'That means I'm the first ranker so I will definitely be happy.'

Then the teacher turned to another student and asked, 'If you get 95 per cent in your test, will you be happy?'

The student said, 'Yes. Of course, that's a great score.'

The teacher then posed another question, 'What if you're the only

person who got 95 per cent and all of your classmates scored higher percentages than you? Would you still be happy?'

The student realized that he would be the last ranker and said, 'No, I wouldn't be happy.'

The teacher then commented, 'So, your happiness depends on others' scores and not yours! Your happiness seems to be influenced by how others perform!'

One student said, 'What is wrong in feeling like this, Ma'am? Are we not studying to top the class? The topper is the happiest student! Even my parents expect me to get better marks than others. And my classmates will respect me if I score better than them! I feel defeated when my scores are less than others.'

The teacher replied, 'Thanks for your honest expression. Unfortunately, many of your peers, and sometimes even parents and the society, have certain undue expectations from you. They get impressed only when you are in the limelight. Consciously or unconsciously, you also think, work and aim to fulfil their expectations. We may think we are successful only when they are impressed with our achievements and we end up wanting to be toppers! Does it mean that those who are not toppers are useless?'

The students were silent.

The teacher said, 'I will explain, but before that, let me ask you another simple question.' She pointed out to another student and asked, 'If you get 70 per cent in one test and 78 per cent in the next one, will that make you happy?'

The student wisely responded, 'Yes, of course, because there is an improvement in my score.'

The teacher concluded, 'That's awesome. The lesson is that real happiness is not in outsmarting or defeating others, but in self-improvement. You need not compete with others, rather compete with yourself. Take inspiration from others who are doing better than you, instead of trying to compete with them or defeating them.'

The students realized that they were aspiring for relative happiness by competing with others and not absolute happiness by trying to improve themselves.

The teacher continued, 'Please don't try to succumb to peer pressure or undue societal expectations. Instead of competing with others, focus on your own growth and progress. Everybody has a unique set of abilities to understand and accomplish things. Embrace your uniqueness and celebrate the little victories, knowing that each step forward is a triumph in your own story. What is good for you need not be good for others. What is good for others need not be the best for you.'

The children were impressed. Their faces lit up.

The teacher explained further, 'You can go on a wonderful journey of self-improvement without competing with others. There's no need to feel superior or inferior to anyone else. You're not in a race to be better than others; you're on a quest to become the best version of yourself!'

The teacher added that this quest was like unlocking new levels of one's abilities each day. It wasn't about comparison, envy, or pride. Rather, it was about discovering one's strengths, growing at one's own pace, and enjoying the wonderful adventure of becoming the most fantastic version of oneself! It had nothing to do with being perfect; it was about making progress and enjoying the journey.

Takeaways from the Tale

- Be on a quest for personal growth, and not in a race to defeat others.
- Unhealthy comparisons can lead to unnecessary stress.
- Become the best version of yourself without the burden of comparison.
- You need not be the best, just try to be your best!
- Don't come under the sway of peer pressure or unhealthy competitive spirit.

Inspiration vs. Jealousy

Imagine you really like playing a musical instrument. When you see someone else playing it really well, you can feel two different things. One is feeling happy and inspired, like, 'Wow, I want to get better like them!' That's called inspiration, and it's good for us. It helps us grow and do our best.

The other feeling is when you look at someone playing and think, 'Oh no, they're better than me' or 'I'm better than them.' That can make you feel jealous or too proud, respectively. It doesn't feel good. Such comparisons associated with unhealthy emotions can make your mind stressed or your friendships strained.

It's important to focus on being the best version of ourselves instead of always thinking about who's better or worse. That way, we can be happy and make good friends!

Now, let's explore the dynamics of how unhealthy comparisons can lead to inferiority and superiority complexes.

Inferiority Complex and Envy

An inferiority complex is a mental condition where you consistently feel inadequate, unworthy, or less competent than others. This feeling of inferiority can stem from various factors, such as comparisons with friends, unrealistic standards, past experiences, or societal expectations. Individuals dealing with inferiority complex often harbour a deep-seated belief that they are inherently flawed or inferior to others.

Envy is closely connected to inferiority complex. Those who experience feelings of inferiority may become envious of those they perceive as more successful, competent or accomplished. Envy arises when there is a strong desire to possess qualities or achievements that others may have, leading to feelings of resentment or frustration.

Inferiority complex or envy can significantly impact your emotional and psychological well-being:

- **Low Self-esteem:** Children with an inferiority complex may struggle with low self-esteem and feel that they are not as capable or valuable as their peers. This can hinder their overall confidence and self-worth.
- **Social Withdrawal:** A child with an inferiority complex might be hesitant to engage in social activities or interact with others. Fear of judgment or comparison can lead to isolation and difficulties in forming positive relationships.
- **Academic Challenges:** Feelings of inferiority can affect a child's academic performance. They may be reluctant to participate in class, express their ideas, or take on challenges, fearing failure or criticism.
- **Impact on Mental Health:** Persistent feelings of inferiority can contribute to anxiety, depression, or other mental health issues in children. The stress of constantly comparing themselves to others can be emotionally taxing.

Superiority Complex and Pride

A superiority complex is a mental attitude characterized by our exaggerated beliefs in our own abilities, status, or accomplishments, especially in comparison to others.

People with a superiority complex tend to overestimate their own importance, competence, or intelligence while underestimating the abilities of others. This mindset manifests as a behaviour that conveys a sense of superiority or entitlement.

Pride and arrogance are closely connected to superiority complex. Having a healthy sense of satisfaction in your achievements and not looking down upon others is a beneficial self-belief. However, when that self-belief becomes excessive and evolves into an attitude of superiority, you can become arrogant and over-confident. This spoils your mental health and brings on stress and various unwanted things.

A superiority complex can have the following effects:

- **Lack of Empathy:** A sense of superiority may lead to a lack of empathy towards others. You may find it difficult to understand or appreciate the perspectives and genuine struggles of your peers.
- **Academic Challenges:** While a healthy level of confidence is beneficial for academic success, an inflated sense of superiority may hinder our ability to learn from others, collaborate on projects, or accept constructive feedback. Believing that our ideas are superior can lead to difficulties in compromise and cooperation.
- **Social Isolation:** Due to a superiority complex, we may distance ourselves from our friends. This can result in social isolation and a limited support network.
- **Strained Relationships:** Those who have a superiority complex may struggle to form genuine connections with peers. Their perceived superiority can create barriers, making it challenging to relate to others on an equal footing. They are unable to freely mingle with their classmates and they eventually feel alienated.

So, instead of constantly comparing ourselves with others and feeling a sense of superiority or inferiority complex, or pride or envy, it's best to focus on upgrading ourselves. Focus on personal growth and self-improvement. Unhealthy comparisons lead to unnecessary stress.

Give up Unhealthy Competitive Spirit

If there is a swimming competition between a monkey and a fish, who will win?

If there is a tree climbing competition between a monkey and a fish, who will win?

In the first case, naturally, the fish will be the winner, and in the second case, the monkey will emerge successful.

The lesson in this little example is that it's not necessary to compete with others and be pressurized to do what others are good at.

Be yourself! Staying true to yourself empowers you to make choices aligning with your own values and interests rather than succumbing to external pressures. This is essential for your mental and emotional well-being. Accept and embrace your unique interests, strengths, and qualities, even if they differ from your peers. It helps build self-esteem, confidence, and resilience. You can, thus, navigate the complex social dynamics of childhood and adolescence while building a strong sense of self.

Remember that you're a unique puzzle piece. You don't have to change who you are to fit in the grid. True friends will like you just the way you are. Each puzzle piece is unique, just like you. Your friends are like other pieces of puzzle, and they should fit in the grid with you naturally.

Tips to Rise above Unhealthy Comparisons

Everybody has their own unique set of talents and qualities in which they can excel and become successful. Unnecessary comparisons spoil relationships and increases stress.

Often times, after achieving something significant, witnessing someone else acquire something better can swiftly snatch away your deserved joy. Giving up the habit of comparing yourself to others is essential for discovering the happiness you genuinely deserve.

Lord Krishna advises us in Bhagavad Gita to stick to our duty and not imitate others.

śreyān sva-dharmo viguṇaḥ
para-dharmāt sv-anuṣṭhitāt
sva-dharme nidhanaṁ śreyaḥ
para-dharmo bhayāvahaḥ

It is far better to perform one's own duties even with some shortcomings than performing another's duties perfectly. Imitating others or taking up someone else's duties leads to unnecessary fear or stress.

Bhagavad Gita (3.35)

This verse from the Gita teaches us that it's important to be ourselves, instead of always trying to imitate someone else. When we try to improve ourselves, it makes us happier and more successful in the long run. Sometimes, we compare ourselves to others, but that can make things confusing and stop us from being our true selves. We all have our own special path and things to learn. It's like having our own exciting adventure!

Here are some effective ways to thwart this thief of comparison and reclaim the happiness that is rightfully yours!

- **Convert Envy into Appreciation:** Instead of envying someone who performed better than you, try to appreciate them for their good qualities and achievements. That mitigates inferiority complex and envy and fosters healthy relationships.
- **Convert Pride into Gratitude:** Instead of feeling bloated on account of your achievements, sincerely thank all those who have supported and helped you become successful. Thus, you can happily celebrate your success without looking down upon anyone. This also mitigates superiority complex and pride and fosters good friendships.
- **Journalling:** Write down your thoughts, feelings, and achievements to create a personal record of your journey. Reflecting on your own experiences can shift the focus from external comparisons to internal growth.
- **Regulating Social Media Usage:** Social media often promotes unrealistic standards and fosters unhealthy comparison or competition. Limit your time on social media platforms and be mindful of how they can impact your self-perception. Try to spend time with people in person.
- **Learning from Others:** Instead of comparing, use others as a source of inspiration. Learn from their experiences and achievements, understanding that everyone's journey is unique.
- **New Hobbies:** Invest time in learning new things, whether through formal education, online courses or self-study. This can shift the focus from external comparisons to personal development.

By using these techniques we can live a blissful life free from the disease of comparison!

One who constantly compares oneself with others also tends to compete with others. Unhealthy competitive spirit and constant attempt to outsmart and defeat others creates stress. Sometimes, such competing tendency is also influenced by peer pressure. Read the next chapter to understand the dynamics of peer pressure, competition related stress and how to deal with them.

TRY THIS OUT!

THE SUCCESS JAR

Get a jar and some colourful papers. Whenever you achieve something, no matter how small, write it down on a piece of paper and put it in the jar. Encourage friends or family to do the same. Over time, the jar becomes a collection of personal victories. When you're feeling the urge to compare yourself with others, take a moment to read the successes in the jar. It's a delightful reminder of your unique journey and accomplishments, shifting the focus from comparison to personal growth and joy.

4 Peer Pressure? Just Embrace Your Uniqueness

The Unhappy Crow

Once upon a time, in a distant forest, there lived a crow. He was happy with his sleek black feathers and the peaceful days spent flying around the green canopy. He was also proud of his beauty and qualities. One fine day, as the crow was soaring through the trees, he saw a regal swan. The crow's world took an unexpected turn; his pride was crushed.

The swan was a vision of beauty, with feathers as white as freshly fallen snow. The crow couldn't help but be captivated by the swan's elegance. Feeling a bit self-conscious about his own black plumage, the crow expressed his admiration, saying, 'You must be the happiest bird in the forest because you are so beautiful.'

The swan, however, humbly replied, 'If you think I am the most beautiful, you haven't seen a parrot yet. He boasts two magnificent colours, unlike my plain white feathers.' With those words, the swan gracefully glided away, leaving the crow contemplating the parrot's vibrant hues.

Days later, as the crow continued his explorations, he saw the parrot. Mesmerized by the parrot's dazzling colours, he exclaimed, 'You must be the happiest bird in the forest.'

The parrot sighed and shared, 'I used to be a very happy bird until I saw the peacock. Its array of colours far surpasses mine as I have only two.' With that, the

parrot fluttered away, leaving the crow curious about the renowned peacock.

Driven by curiosity, the crow flew beyond the familiar forest, seeking the peacock. Finally, after a long journey, he discovered the magnificent bird. The peacock's vibrant feathers spread like a living rainbow, captivating everyone around. The crow approached in awe and spoke, 'You must be the happiest bird alive. Your colours and feathers are truly magnificent and so many people admire you.'

The peacock, however, revealed a different truth, 'How can I be happy about my colours when I am trapped in this zoo, unable to roam freely? Sometimes, I wish I were a crow. You, my friend, are the only bird who is not caged, and I would trade these colours for some freedom any day.'

In that moment, the crow learnt a valuable lesson—comparing himself to others was not right. Each bird had its own blessings, and his freedom was a treasure that no vibrant plumage could replace. With newfound gratitude, the crow returned to his forest home, cherishing the unique beauty of his black feathers and the freedom that set him apart.

Takeaways from the Tale

- Don't be too proud of your own qualities; there might always be someone better than you.
- Don't be sad that you don't have what others have; be happy with what you have.
- Everyone is gifted in a unique way; be grateful for what you have and what you are.
- Don't be proud or envious of anyone; everyone has something to celebrate.

Peer Pressure

Peer pressure is the influence exerted by one's peers or social circle to conform to their attitudes, behaviours, or expectations. It can come in many forms, such as the pressure to dress a certain way, play certain games, go for particular outings, adopt specific interests, or even engage in risky behaviours.

For example, you may be someone who enjoys reading and painting, but you become part of a peer group that's heavily into sports. You may feel the pressure to join the school's football team, despite your disinterest, because you may be concerned about losing friends if you don't comply. This peer pressure can lead to stress and inner conflict. If one comes under peer pressure or societal expectations, they constantly try to impress people around them and thus miss on their own genuine interests, talents, and tastes.

Self-imposed Peer Pressure

Problem: At times, peer pressure isn't solely about external expectations placed upon us by our peers. It can also be an internal influence that stems from our own desire to conform for social acceptance. Just like the crow felt the pressure to look beautiful, we might feel the need to measure up, even if nobody is pointing fingers at us. This self-imposed stress and pressure can have negative effects.

Solution: To navigate this complex dynamic, it's essential to introspect deeply, to identify your true nature, strengths, and weaknesses. Rather than striving to mimic others, recognize and embrace the unique talents and abilities that you possess as God's gifts. Just like the crow, every individual is blessed with distinct qualities, and we need to acknowledge and honour these individual strengths.

Don't Try to Impress Others

Little Hari liked to play the violin and was exceptionally good at it. However, his friends made fun of him for playing a 'classical' instrument, calling it uncool. Despite peer pressure, Hari continued practising the violin because it was his true passion. Over time, his dedication to being himself not only led him to achieve several musical feats but also earned him respect from his peers when they saw his confidence and the beauty in what he did.

Peer pressure can manifest when peers single us out and try to make us someone we're not or don't want to be. At that time, instead of trying to fit in or please others, we should focus on staying true to ourselves and developing our unique strengths. By doing this, we not only remain authentic but also contribute to a diverse and vibrant community that celebrates everyone's individuality.

CAUTION: It's awesome to be yourself, but it's also important to learn good things from others. Being yourself is great, but that shouldn't be done out of arrogance and a strong sense of self-righteousness. Imagine you have friends and classmates who do great things. You can still be yourself, but it's okay to pick up good habits from them. That way, you can grow and have better relationships with everyone!

Don't Create Peer Pressure: It's important to not let others make you do things that are not possible for you to do. And it's equally important that you don't make your friends or classmates do such things either. Of course, as friends we need to extend ourselves to accommodate each other's interests. But we also need to respect each other's nature and preferences, and cooperatively co-exist. When someone needs their space, it's nice to give it to them and not push them into something they can't do or don't like to do.

Remember, we're all different,

and that's natural and cool! We should respect this and be kind to each other, just the way we are, while improving ourselves in the right way.

Being true to yourself and respecting others for who they are can help us have less stress and make life happier for everyone. But what if others criticize or bully you unnecessarily? The next chapter answers this question.

TRY THIS OUT!

POSITIVE APPRECIATION CIRCLE

Sit in a circle with friends or family members, and one by one, share a positive quality about the person on your right. Emphasize the importance of focusing on character traits, kindness, and strengths. This activity not only promotes a positive and uplifting atmosphere, but also helps recognize and appreciate the unique qualities in each other. It shifts the attention from comparison to building each other with encouraging words.

5 Criticism and Bullying? Seek Help

Lily's Joy and Sorrow!

Lily was known for her cheerful personality and always wore a bright smile on her face. She had a best friend named Rani, and together, they were inseparable.

Once, Lily had to work on a school project with her classmate, Rani. They were so excited and full of pleasant emotions as they gathered their art supplies, giggling about their grand ideas. Lily felt a warm feeling in her heart because Rani appreciated her ideas and was always there to support her.

However, things took an unexpected turn when Lily had to join forces with another classmate named Ruchi, who had a reputation for being somewhat discouraging. She passed unkind remarks about Lily's creative ideas for the project. The warm emotions Lily had felt earlier with Rani quickly turned into bitter ones when she worked with Ruchi. She felt hurt and disappointed by her negative comments.

Lily couldn't hide her feelings anymore. She shared her experience with her father. 'Dad, I feel very joyful with Rani. But my happiness turns into sadness when I have to deal with Ruchi. I feel so stressed and in pain.' Tears welled up in her eyes as she expressed her emotions, 'I love Rani, and I hate Ruchi.'

Lily's father listened carefully, his warm and reassuring presence making Lily feel better. He then gently explained, 'Dear child, in our interactions with people around us, our minds experience fear, anger, happiness, sadness, surprise, and disgust. When someone appreciates us or praises our work, we feel encouraged, and our minds store a positive impression of that person. We want to be around them and feel enlivening vibrations. However, when someone criticizes, scolds, or discourages us, our minds store negative impressions, making us want to distance ourselves from them.'

Lily nodded and said, 'Yes, Rani appreciates and encourages me, but Ruchi criticizes and discourages me.'

Lily's father replied, 'These emotions in your mind are natural responses to how people deal with you. But it's not worth dwelling on these negative feelings for a long time. You shouldn't allow others to influence your emotions so much. You need to be strong from within.'

Lily innocently asked, 'How can I be strong?'

Dad said lovingly, 'Simple! You don't need to take every remark seriously. If Ruchi's comments are valid, accept them. If her words are invalid, ignore them. If she is pointing out some genuine faults in your work, she is actually helping you to improve yourself. Take it positively for your betterment. Through her comments, you can understand where you went wrong and can work on it.'

Lily said, 'Yes, some faults that she pointed out were valid. But my point is that the way she speaks is very rude. Instead of helping me improve my faults, she discourages me.'

Dad replied, 'I understand! It's painful. Try to ignore her intentions and only acknowledge her words!'

Lily never saw the situation from this angle. She never thought that *words* and *intentions* can be seen separately. She wiped her tears and hugged her father tightly. She realized that her father's wise words would help her deal with different kinds of people better. Basically, her dad was trying to make her emotionally resilient. Lily learnt to appreciate the warmth in her heart when she was with friends like Rani and not let negative emotions bring her down.

Finally, Lily's dad advised her, 'But mind you, my dear, hate the sin, not the sinner! Ruchi might have been rude to you, but if you deal with her without hating her, it's quite possible that she would be your good friend in no time. But if that doesn't happen, then you can escalate the matter to your teacher or to me.' Lily thought about it for a moment and decided to give it a try.

The next day, Lily went to school, equipped with more courage. And as usual, Ruchi started bullying her. However, Lily ignored it and didn't get emotional like before.

Ruchi was surprised. The next day, she gathered a few more kids and made fun of Lily's appearance and called her hurtful names. Lily thought of being patient and tolerant as per her father's advice.

Yet Lily felt uncomfortable and anxious. Gradually, she became stressed every morning, dreading the thought of going to school and facing the bullies. She couldn't focus on her studies and the project because her mind was preoccupied with fear.

One day, Ruchi and her group became extremely rude with her. Lily thought that things were crossing limits. She informed her dad about the bullying she had been facing in greater detail now. Then her dad said, 'Lily, if people's mistakes are small and incidental, you may tolerate and forgive them. But if they purposely try to bully you, you must take an action. I'm glad that you spoke to me. Tomorrow, I will come to your school.'

The next day, her dad went and spoke to the class teacher and the school principal, and together they put a stop to the bullies' behaviour. Lily started feeling better and the stress slowly faded away. Those who bullied her learnt a lesson, and gradually became her friends.

Seeking help and talking to someone she trusted made all the difference in Lily's life. Just like seeing a doctor when you're sick, sharing our problems with relevant people helps us feel better.

Takeaways from the Tale

- Appreciation and supportive friends energize us.
- Criticism can sometimes contain valuable insights for personal improvement.
- Learn to separate people's words from their intentions. Take the essence of both.
- Negativity exists, but you have to choose not to dwell on negative emotions.
- In the name of tolerance and forgiveness, we need not allow ourselves to be troubled so much.
- Effective communication can ease stress in social circles.

General Criticism

In this world, sometimes people appreciate us and sometimes, criticize us, too. If the appreciation is genuine, we can take it as encouragement and be happy. If the criticism is valid, we can take it as feedback for self-improvement, and work on it.

But sometimes we receive exaggerated praise or unnecessary criticism. Taking praise too seriously can make us proud. And taking

criticism too seriously can make us demotivated. So, we need to be wise enough to understand it and not get overly affected by it.

Wise people are unaffected by undue praise or unnecessary criticism; they focus on their priorities. Therefore, Lord Krishna says in the Bhagavad Gita:

tulya-nindā-stutir maunī
santuṣhṭo yena kenachit
aniketaḥ sthira-matir
bhaktimān me priyo naraḥ

Those who are equipoised in praise and criticism, satisfied within, unattached to the different places, and maintain a steady mind, are very dear to Me.

Bhagavad Gita 12.19

Attaining this mindset may take some time, but ultimately, we all must try to reach that maturity.

Dealing with Bullying

It's common that we are sometimes troubled by people around us. If someone accidentally troubles you slightly, you may excuse that person and show some tolerance and kindness. But if someone is troubling you purposely, you shouldn't keep quiet, but take an appropriate action.

'Bullying' is when someone repeatedly says or does hurtful things to you on purpose. It can make you feel scared, sad, or stressed. When someone is being bullied, they might constantly worry about what might happen next or feel anxious to go to school or being around certain people.

If someone is repeatedly unkind to you, immediately tell a trusted grown-up, like a parent or a teacher. They can take the necessary steps to address the bullying.

Speaking up is not a sign of weakness; it's a sign of courage. It's like asking for help when you're not feeling well.

So, if you're ever being bullied or know someone who is, remember, it's important to seek help from a trusted adult. They can support you, protect you, and help you overcome the stress and fear caused by bullying.

And please remember, not to bully anyone or make negative remarks about them. Just as you are pained by someone's misbehaviour with you, they will also feel similar pain if you do the same.

Learn to empathize with others. Treat others the way you would like to be treated.

Tools to Deal with Criticism and Bullying

By applying the following effective tools, you can be relieved from the stress caused by criticism and bullying.

1. **Positive Friendship:** It's always wonderful to have friends like Rani who make you feel happy, appreciated, encouraged, and supported. Being around such friends can fill your heart with joy and positive energy. Such positive vibrations energize us.

2. **Stay Away from Sources of Negativity:** Sometimes, you might meet people like Ruchi who say unkind things or discourage you. It can be hurtful and make you sad. You need not hate them but be careful in your dealings with them. Don't be overly affected by their negative comments. It's not worth losing focus on your goals by giving attention to things unworthy of our time and mind space.
3. **Choose your Reaction:** You can choose how you react to what people say. You can take their good advice and ignore the bad intentions. This makes you strong from within. But if they tend to harm you, of course, you must do the needful to protect yourself by taking help from relevant people.
4. **Separate Words from Intentions:** Sometimes, people say things in a rude manner, but their words might have some truth in them. Don't fail to focus on their valid points and try to ignore their

intentions as much as possible. Those words, although spoken maliciously, can reveal our shortcomings and help us grow.

5. **Hate the Sin, Not the Sinner:** It's important to not hate people, even if they are unkind. Try to be patient and understand them. They might change themselves by observing your kind dealings and you could even become friends one day.
6. **Sharing Feelings:** It's important to talk to someone you trust, like Lily did with her father. Sharing your feelings with well-wishers and elders can make you feel better and get a new perspective of the situation at hand. Family and friends can provide love and guidance to help you navigate your feelings and make you stronger.
7. **Seek Help:** Sharing your pains and emotions with trusted ones can help you feel better. But sometimes the situation can be so delicate that mere expression of feelings may not solve the problem; it needs action. So, when the extent of criticism or bullying crosses tolerable limits, immediately seek help from an elder—a teacher or a parent—who can intervene and do the needful.

Learn to manage your emotions and reactions to different people and make your friendships and relationships more positive and fulfilling.

What happens when we expect a certain outcome but receive unexpected results? What can we do about this? Well, let's find out in the next chapter.

TRY THIS OUT!

Maintain a 'Magical Mindfulness Diary' where you can do the following:

Magical Mindfulness Diary

Reflect on Advice	Journal about recent constructive advice you've received. Explore its potential impact on personal growth.
Identify Harmful Influences	Recall negative instances or harmful intentions. Outline strategies to distance yourself from such influences.
Cultivate Strength	List personal strengths and past successes. Reflect on how these strengths can be applied in current situations.
Seek Support	Share your reflections with trusted friends or mentors. Seek help on navigating challenges and reinforcing positive behaviours.
Learn and Grow	Embrace a growth mindset. Journal the lessons learnt and apply them to future situations.

Making these activities a part of your routine can help you understand more about yourself, become stronger when facing challenges, and keep a happy and positive outlook on things.

6 Unexpected Results? Cultivate Detachment!

Dutiful Work with Detachment

Once in a cheerful village, there was a young boy named Aryan who loved to paint. Aryan dreamt of creating a masterpiece that would make everyone in the village admire his talent. With each stroke of his brush, he imagined the praise and recognition he would receive.

One day, an elderly artist named Nataraja visited the village. Intrigued by Aryan's talent, he appreciated him and taught him some special techniques to paint in a better manner.

Inspired by Nataraja's wisdom, Aryan decided to paint a mural for the upcoming village festival. He worked tirelessly, pouring his heart into every detail. As the festival approached, Aryan found himself imagining the admiration and applause he would receive.

When the day of the festival arrived, Aryan proudly unveiled his mural. The villagers were indeed impressed by his skill, but Aryan noticed that not everyone reacted as he had expected. Some praised, while others had different opinions.

Feeling a mix of emotions, Aryan talked to Nataraja about it. He said, 'Sir, I tried all the special tricks you taught me but not everyone loved my painting.' Aryan was looking very sad because he failed to meet the results that he had expected.

Seeing the little child's sadness, Nataraja reminded him of the Gita's wisdom and said, 'Dear Aryan, it's okay. Having dreams and working hard is great but expecting everyone to love it might make you sad. The joy is in creating, not just in what people think. Do your best, but don't worry too much about what happens.' He further added, 'Your painting is exquisite, and your dedication is evident. Please remember that the joy is in creating something beautiful, not just in winning a prize.'

From that day forward, Aryan painted with love and dedication, finding fulfilment in the process rather than the results.

Taking Nataraja's advice to heart, Aryan decided to paint for the sheer joy of creating, without expecting specific reactions. He continued to paint murals for various events, putting his best effort into each one.

Over time, Aryan's detached approach allowed him to grow as an artist. People began to appreciate his work even more because they could sense the authenticity and determination in his creations.

The village celebrated Aryan as a wise artist, teaching everyone that while having dreams and working hard was important, finding joy in the process and remaining detached from outcomes was the true essence of a fulfilling life.

Takeaways from the Tale

- Find joy in the creative process, not just in the outcomes.
- Dreams and hard work are valuable, but universal praise may not be guaranteed.
- Constructive criticism is an opportunity for growth.
- Wisdom from elders guides to a healthy balance between effort and detachment.
- Authenticity matters; detachment allows sincerity to shine through.

Balancing Effort and Detachment

Imagine you are getting ready for a football match. You can practise your kicks, work on your dribbling skills, and be in the best shape possible for the game. But once the game starts, you don't know exactly how the other team will play or what the final score will be. That's a bit like preparing for an exam!

- **Prepare with Dedication:** Just like practising for a game, preparing for an exam means studying, doing your homework, and understanding the lessons your teacher has taught you. It's in your hands to put in the effort and be ready for whatever questions might come up.

- **Do your Best:** When you play a game, you give it your all, right? The same goes for exams. You want to do your best and show what you've learned. Answering the questions to the best of your ability is your goal during the exam.
- **Detach yourself from Results:** Now, here's the interesting part. After the football game, you might win, lose or have a tie. Similarly, after the exam, you might get a great score, an average score or even score poorly. While you can control how well you prepare and perform, you can't control what kind of questions will be on the exam or how it will be graded.
- **Enjoy the Process:** Just like one should enjoy playing the game, one should enjoy the process of learning and preparing for the exam as well. Learning new things can be fun and interesting! When you are focused on understanding and enjoying what you are learning, it makes the whole experience more enjoyable.
- **Learn and Grow:** Whether you win or lose a game or get a high or low score on an exam, what matters most is what you learn from the experience. Each game and each exam is a chance to grow and become better. You might learn new strategies for the next game or discover new study techniques for the next exam.

The Art of Smart Work

Lord Krishna teaches us a golden lesson in the Bhagavad Gita:

karmaṇy evādhikāras te
mā phaleṣu kadācana
mā karma-phala-hetur bhūr
mā te saṅgo 'stv akarmaṇi

This verse has four parts:

1. *You have a right to perform your duty*
2. *You are not entitled to the results*
3. *Never consider yourself the cause of the results of your activities*
4. *Never give up your duties or responsibilities*

This means, focus on doing your best (your duties), but don't worry too much about what happens after (the fruits). This ancient wisdom teaches us to perform our responsibilities with dedication but remain detached from the outcomes.

Bhagavad Gita (2.47)

When we dream big about what we want to do and how others will see us, we put a heavy load of expectations on ourselves that is hard to carry. It's great to have plans and dreams, and it's healthy to put in a lot of effort to achieve them. However, after giving our best, it's crucial to take a step back, disconnect, and not get too attached to the outcome. When our plans become expectations, we make ourselves vulnerable to feeling unhappy. When our expectations are not repeatedly met, we can become depressed; and when they are, we can become arrogant.

So, let's give our best effort in preparing and enjoying the learning process, and let the results take care of themselves!

Causes of Anger

In a beautiful village, there once lived a girl named Sonia, having a heart as bright as the traditional fabrics she wore, had a tiny spark of anger often flickered within her, turning even the simplest moments into stormy clouds.

What's Wrong with Anger?

In relation to anger, Lord Krishna says in the Bhagavad Gita (16.21):

tri-vidhaṁ narakasyedaṁ
dvāraṁ nāśanam ātmanaḥ
kāmaḥ krodhas tathā lobhas
tasmād etat trayaṁ tyajet

There are three gates leading to this hell—desire, anger, and greed. Every sane person should give up these qualities, for they lead to degradation.

Bhagavad Gita (16.21)

One day, after a particularly stressful episode, Sonia decided that this was getting too much. She approached her dear grandfather for a solution.

Grandpa was resting under a tall tree. Sonia approached him and poured her heart out, explaining how tiny frustrations were turning into storms of anger, causing her a great deal of stress.

Grandpa listened intently; his eyes filled with understanding. 'Sonia, my dear,' he said, 'anger is like a wild river that, if left unchecked, can drown the beauty of everything around it. To be free from stress, you must let go of this anger, like releasing a red balloon into the sky.'

Perplexed but eager to find peace, Sonia asked, 'But Grandpa, how do I give up my anger?'

Grandpa beamed warmly and shared a timeless piece of wisdom: 'When we really want something or expect things to happen our way, and they don't, we often get angry. It's similar to really wanting a toy, and when you don't get it, you get upset. Or when you think someone should behave in a certain way, and they don't, you can get really angry or annoyed.'

Sonia said, 'Yes, that's correct.'

Grandpa continued, 'So, the best way to enjoy life is to live it the way it is going. Don't intensely desire to have something. Don't always expect specific reactions from people. Many times, our expectations are not met which can make us angry or sad. It's great to have some small wishes, but if we have too many of those and expect all of them to get fulfilled, we set ourselves up for failure. So, dear Sonia, learn to regulate the number of your wishes and expectations and then see how magically your anger will run away.'

From that day on, Sonia carefully kept a watch over her wants and gradually reduced her undue expectations from others. Magically, her angry disposition reduced as well!

Takeaways from the Tale

- Unfulfilled desires and expectations are the two causes of anger.
- Self-awareness is the catalyst for personal growth.
- Seeking guidance enhances problem-solving.
- Letting go of intense desires leads to inner peace.
- Managing expectations reduces stress and anger.

Regulating Desires and Expectations

Giving an amazing solution to anger, Lord Krishna says in the Bhagavad Gita (2.70):

> ***āpūryamāṇam acala-pratiṣṭhaṁ***
> ***samudram āpaḥ praviśanti yadvat***
> ***tadvat kāmā yaṁ praviśanti sarve***
> ***sa śāntim āpnoti na kāma-kāmī***

> *A person who is not disturbed by the incessant flow of desires—that enter like rivers into the ocean, which is ever being filled but is always still—can alone achieve peace, and not the man who strives to satisfy such desires.*
>
> Bhagavad Gita (2.70)

Imagine your mind is like a calm and peaceful ocean, and your wishes are like rivers flowing into it. It's totally fine to have wishes, like wanting a cool toy or yummy treats. But if we want more things all the time, it will feel like too many rivers rushing into our calm ocean.

So, Lord Krishna suggests something amazing: The superhero secret to feeling peaceful and stress-free is to enjoy the things you already have! It's like having a special power that fills you with happiness and delight. You can still have wishes, just not too many all the time. It's like having a super cool strategy to keep your mind happy and delightful at all times!

Tools to Control Anger

- **Chant a Mantra:** Chant your favourite mantra like—'*Om namo bhagavata vasudevaya*' or '*Om namo narayanaya*'—to help control your anger. You not only calm down, but also invoke spiritual blessings that can help you feel empowered to manage the situation at hand.
- **Talk about It:** Share why you're upset with someone you trust—a friend, a family member, or even a pet. Talking about it helps the anger go away.
- **Draw or Write:** Grab your drawing kit and a piece of paper. Draw or write about your feelings. Thus, you can divert your attention to something simple, positive, and productive.

Is Anger Always Bad?

Anger is not always bad. Sometimes, anger has its utility in rectifying a situation. When you are dealing with people who only listen to you when you say it assertively, you may have to assert and emphasize to make your point.

For example, Hanuman became angry with Ravana for his grave offence of kidnapping Sita. Consequently, Hanuman burnt the whole of Lanka, the golden city of Ravana. Another example is of Arjuna, who directed his anger towards the wicked supporters of Duryodhana in the battle of Kurukshetra. While acts of violence can't be justified, punishments stemming from anger can teach a lesson to the arrogant. But it's important to ensure that you don't come under the sway of anger for too long and lose your composure.

Exhibit controlled resistance if needed, but don't come under the control of anger.

TRY THIS OUT!

Make a list of all the things like toys, treats, or games that you really want. Now, you have a whole week to try and get all of them.

The following week, create a new list by reflecting on what you really need, like something that helps you. For example, stationery for school or props for a play. Try to get all those things.

Notice how you feel at the end of the first week when you try to get everything you want but can't. Did you feel frustrated, or a bit upset?

Now, in the second week, when you focus on getting what you actually need, reflect on how you felt. Was there more contentment and satisfaction? Highlight these differences.

By embarking on this little adventure, we can ascertain the benefits of focusing on what we truly need versus what we simply want.

Magical Tools for Mindfulness

SECTION 2

In the previous section, we explored how our minds work in tandem with the gross senses and the subtle intelligence and ego.

In this section, we will explore some traditional tools to practise mindfulness which have been adopted since ages. These practical and effective methods will undoubtedly help you shift from distraction to concentration and distress to de-stress.

Just like our bodies need exercise and nourishment, our minds benefit from activities like mantra meditation and journalling our feelings. This section connects with what we learnt earlier and explores breathing techniques, exercises and meditation to make mindfulness a cool and helpful part of our lives.

1 The Three Modes of Human Behaviour

The Three Fish

In a serene lake, three fish, namely Sat, Raj and Tam, resided. Each of them embodied distinct qualities.

Sat was a fish of wisdom and serenity. He approached life with a thoughtful and disciplined demeanour, ever observant of his surroundings. He was a master of planning and remained resolute in the face of challenges.

Raj, on the other hand, was restless and impulsive. His actions were often hasty and aggressive, driven by the urgency of the moment.

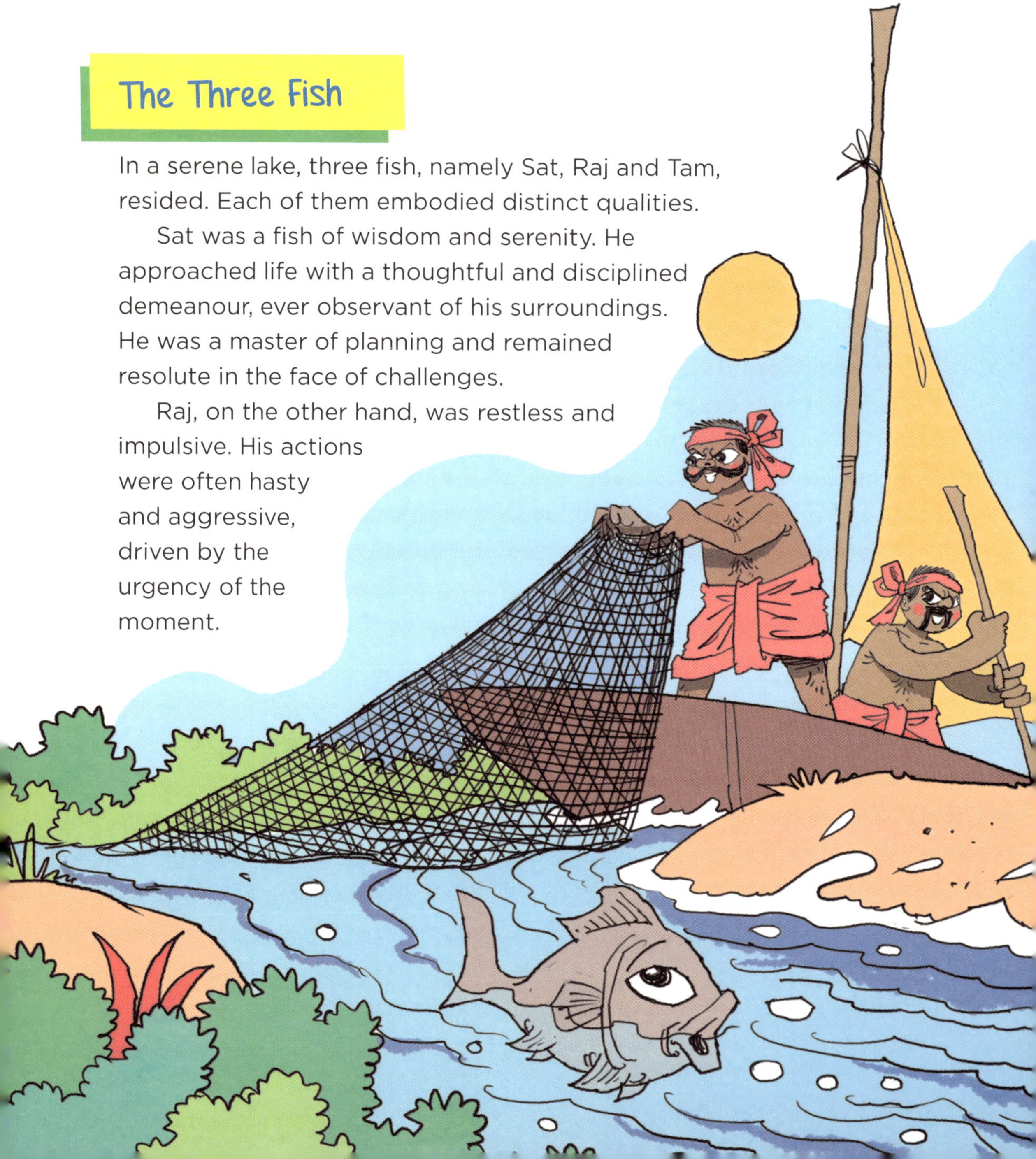

Tam, the third fish, was sluggish and attached to the comfort of routine, reluctant to embrace change. Confusion and inactivity were his companions.

One fateful day, a group of fishermen arrived at the lake with the intention of capturing the fish and earning profits.

Sat, ever watchful, overheard the fishermen's ominous discussions and quickly devised a plan. He knew of a small stream that connected the lake to a vast river and decided to make his escape before the fishermen returned. He informed Raj and Tam about the impending danger, but they paid little heed to his warning. With a composed mind, Sat swam away, reaching the safety of the river before the fishermen arrived.

When the fishermen's nets descended into the lake, Raj remembered Sat's words and panicked. Frantically, he darted around, narrowly evading the encroaching net. His impulsive actions left him exhausted and frustrated, but by a stroke of luck, he managed to find the stream's outlet and escaped into the river.

For Tam, the challenge was totally bewildering. He attempted to hide in a corner of the lake to secure himself. Unfortunately, his ignorance and resistance to adapt proved costly as he got captured in the net, meeting a tragic fate.

Takeaways from the Tale

- Wisdom and planning lead to successful navigation of challenges.
- Adaptability is crucial in overcoming unforeseen obstacles.
- Ignoring warnings may have consequences; value good advice.
- Different approaches to life yield varied outcomes in difficulties.
- Foresight and preparation mitigate risks and enhance survival outcomes.

The Three Modes

This tale of the three fish serves as a parable for how the three *gunas* influence our responses to life's challenges. *Sattva* (wisdom and clarity) enables effective decision-making, *rajas* (passion and restlessness) can lead to frenetic actions, and *tamas* (ignorance and laziness) often results in a lack of self-preservation. These three modes are represented by the three fish—Sat, Raj and Tam.

People predominantly influenced by sattva can face challenges with maturity, even transforming negative stress into a catalyst for personal growth. Those under the sway of rajas may struggle or sometimes succeed with great effort in the face of challenges. And those influenced by tamas are mostly at a disadvantage.

These are the natural forces to this world that impel human beings to act in various ways, and thus experience happiness, distress, stress and so on. These forces affect how we think and behave, leading to good or not-so-good outcomes.

1. **Sattva (Goodness):** Sattva is like a bright and clear mind. It represents goodness, wisdom, and happiness. The minds and intelligence of those who are in

sattva are bright like the Sun. Such people can see things clearly and understand them better.

2. **Rajas (Passion):** Rajas is like a super busy and hyperactive mind. It represents strong desire and intense attachment. It is also the force that makes us want things and gives us the energy to chase our desires. Those who are in rajas are ambitious and work hard for their achievements. They take great pleasure in their accomplishments.
3. **Tamas (Ignorance):** Tamas is like a sleepy and lazy mind. It represents darkness and confusion. The minds of those who are influenced by tamas are confused and weak. Such people are ignorant of their own welfare and perform deeds without knowledge and wisdom, often harming themselves.

It is evident that sattva is the best, tamas is the worst, and rajas is in between. The influence of three forces is spread all over the world. They affect the thoughts and actions of almost everyone. By understanding their functions, we can work towards having more sattva (goodness and wisdom) in our lives and reduce the impact of rajas (passion and desire) and tamas (ignorance and confusion). This helps us become better and happier individuals.

Stress and the Three Modes

These three gunas are connected to stress in the following ways:

1. **Sattva and Stress Reduction:** As sattva represents qualities like clarity, wisdom, and inner peace, a predominance of sattva can help reduce stress in your life. A calm and balanced mind can handle challenging situations more effectively and is less likely to become overwhelmed by stress.
2. **Rajas and Stress Creation:** As rajas represents qualities like desire, restlessness, and attachment, when you have too much rajas in your life, it can lead to negative stress. Excessive desires,

constant restlessness, and attachments can create a sense of unease and dissatisfaction, contributing to stress.

3. **Tamas and Stress Amplification:** As tamas represents qualities like ignorance, laziness, and confusion, when it is prominent enough, it can increase stress. Ignorance and confusion can make you feel helpless or lost in stressful situations, while laziness can prevent you from taking necessary actions to alleviate stress.

Therefore, an imbalanced presence of rajas and tamas in your life can lead to negative stress, while cultivating more sattva can help reduce stress by promoting clarity, wisdom, and inner peace. Balancing these gunas and focusing on sattva can be a helpful way to manage and reduce stress in your life. This aligns with the idea of striving for a more harmonious and balanced existence, as taught in the Bhagavad Gita:

'To effectively cope with stress, we must transcend the influences of rajas and tamas and cultivate the qualities of sattva in our lives.'

Those who are overly under the influence of rajas and tamas are overly affected by stress. Those who are in sattva also face stressful situations, but can maturely deal with them. The next chapter talks about the complex causes of stress and the resultant symptoms which are products of rajas and tamas. We will also discuss several practices that help us cultivate sattva.

TRY THIS OUT!

We've got an exciting activity that can help you uncover your very own gunas—the special qualities that make you unique! Let's dive in and discover them!

Below is a list of fifteen questions. Tick whichever option suits you the best.

QUESTION	A	B	C
Q1. What time do you wake up?	5.00-6.30 a.m.	6.30-8.00 a.m.	8.00-9.30 a.m.
Q2. How truthful are you?	Always try to be truthful	Variable. Depends on the situation	Lie quite often
Q3. How much do you try to help others and not be self-centred?	Mostly all the time	Sometimes	Rarely
Q4. How frequently do you get angry?	Rarely	Occasionally	Frequently
Q5. When things don't go as planned, you might ...	... find the positive side of the situation.	... get upset and want things to be different.	... carelessly ignore the situation.
Q6. How forgiving are you?	Quite forgiving	Need to make an effort to forgive others	Can't forgive; usually build grudges against people
Q7. How would you describe your cleanliness habits?	Your room is always clean and tidy	Sometimes clean and sometimes out of place	Your room is mostly in a shabby place
Q8. When I really want something that is not good for me ...	... I usually resist because I'm strong.	... I try to make good choices but mostly fail.	... I always fail and I'm not eager to improve.
Q9. Where do you find yourself most often?	In the present moment	In the future, contemplating goals, etc.	In the past, reflecting on incidents and memories
Q10. How do you approach work?	Without being too focused on the results	Often seeking results and rewards for my efforts	Prefer not to work; I'd rather relax

Q11. When confronted with a challenge or unfamiliar situation, what do you do?	You stay resourceful and calm	You somehow try to address it	You will rather curse the situation that you are in
Q12. How would you describe your speech?	Sober, peaceful and calming	A bit aggressive	Dull, low sounding or confusing
Q13. What music do you prefer listening to?	Soothing melodies	Loud and fast songs	Sad and tragic tunes
Q14. What is your guiding principle in life?	Accept and go with the flow	Strive to succeed	Ignorance is bliss
Q15. How do you generally behave with your family?	Calm, composed and cheerful	Tend to be moody and get angry frequently	Usually irritated and dull

These questions will help you check which of the three gunas is prominent in you. If mostly 'A's suit your personality the best, you are predominantly in sattva-guna. If it's mostly 'B's, your prominent mode is rajas-guna, and 'C's belong to tamas-guna. 'A's are the best, but 'B's, are not always bad, and many 'C's indicate that you have a long way to stress less and concentrate on important things.

Generally, no one in this world can be in sattva-guna all the time. All of us are influenced by a little bit of rajas and tamas. So, don't worry about being perfect. Target to reduce 'C's by cultivating the habits of sattva and minimize the influence of the other two. Sattvic qualities make you a beacon of positivity and tranquility. Rajasic spirit adds dynamism to your super adventures, but you need to keep its negative traits in control. Tamas makes you lazy and confused, so you need to strive to overcome it.

2 Balance and Regulation

Regulate to Rejuvenate

In a quaint village surrounded by lush fields, there lived a young farmer named Nanda. Nanda was known for his hard work and dedication, but he often found himself stressed and overwhelmed by the demanding nature of his work and the unpredictable challenges of farming. He missed joyful moments with his family and friends due to his super busy activities. He would even compromise on eating and sleeping while being ambitious at work.

One day, Nanda was sitting under a banyan tree, tired from the day's events. As he sat there perspiring in exhaustion, a wise sage

approached him. The sage was known for his deep understanding of life's intricacies.

'Nanda,' the sage said, 'your commitment to your farm is commendable, but like anyone, you need some rest. You cannot keep on working. To thrive in your work, you must find balance in all aspects of your life. Just imagine exercising only one arm for a long time. That arm may appear strong and muscular, but the rest of the body will remain weak, won't it?'

Intrigued, Nanda listened as the sage shared his insights. The sage explained, 'Regulated habits in eating, sleeping, work, and recreation could counteract your physical exertion and mental stress. Think of an archer releasing an arrow from his bow. When he places the arrow on the string, he first brings it back. On seeing this anyone might comment, "Why are you pulling the arrow back when it needs to go forward?" However, the archer knows that when he pulls the arrow back, he will get the required support and stability to shoot the arrow at a faster speed, which wouldn't be possible if he didn't pull the string back. Similarly, you need to find some time, relax, and then continue working with rejuvenated energy.'

Nanda realized that his relentless pursuit of work had left him exhausted and drained. Inspired by the sage's words, he decided to bring balance into his life. He started by maintaining a more regular sleep schedule, ensuring he ate nourishing meals, and taking breaks to engage in activities he enjoyed, along with his farming.

As Nanda adopted these changes, he noticed a positive shift in his life. His farm flourished and his mind became clearer.

One day, a severe storm hit the village, threatening to destroy the crops. Nanda, with his newfound strength and balance, took strategic measures to protect his fields. While other exhausted farmers struggled to salvage their crops, Nanda's regulated lifestyle allowed him to think clearly and act decisively. His farm not only survived the storm but also thrived in its aftermath.

The village soon took notice of Nanda's success and sought his advice. Nanda shared the wisdom he had gained from the sage and encouraged others to live a balanced life with the help of regulated pattern of sound sleep, diet, exercise, recreation, prayer, meditation and worship. The village embraced a collective effort to lead more regulated and balanced lives.

Over time, the village flourished, and the once-exhausted farmers found renewed strength. Nanda's journey became a testament to the transformative power of balance and regulation, reminding everyone that in the flow of life, finding equilibrium was the key to resilience and prosperity.

Takeaways from the Tale

- Balance is the key to resilience and prosperity in life.
- Work without rest leads to stress; balance in sleep, diet, and recreation brings strength.
- Regulated lifestyle not only saves but also guides us in facing challenges.
- Wisdom from an archer: Step back, find support, and rejuvenate for greater success.
- Regulated habits bring collective prosperity and strength in the community.

Four Things to Balance

Lord Krishna teaches us the art of regulation and balancing the four basic aspects of life, as suggested in the following verse of Bhagavad Gita:

yuktāhāra-vihārasya
yukta-ceṣṭasya karmasu
yukta-svapnāvabodhasya
yogo bhavati duḥkha-hā

One who is regulated in their habits of eating, sleeping, recreation and work can mitigate all problems and difficulties in life by practising yoga.

Bhagavad Gita (6.17)

Achieving balance in acts of sleeping, eating, recreation, and work is essential for maintaining overall well-being and reducing stress. The art of balancing and regulating these four activities in our daily routine helps us come to the level of sattva and rise above rajas and tamas. Here's an elaboration on each aspect:

1. Balance in Eating

A balanced diet is crucial for sustained energy levels, focus, and overall health. Practise mindful eating by paying attention to hunger and fullness cues. Chew properly for good digestion. Avoid skipping meals to maintain consistent energy throughout the day. Avoid overeating as it can make you sleepy, tired and obese, and also cause indigestion.

Analysing the previous verse of the Bhagavad Gita can help us understand the three types of food that we eat and consciously choose our menu.

- **Sattvic Foods:** Sattvic foods are pure and wholesome. They increase our lifespan and enhance our strength, health and satisfaction. They promote clarity, focus, and overall well-being. Include a variety of fruits, vegetables, whole grains, and nuts in your meals. These foods are not only nutritious but also help in maintaining sustained energy levels. They align with the principle of sattva or purity, fostering a calm and focused mind.
- **Rajasic Foods:** Rajasic foods are those that include spicy or stimulating elements. They are excessively bitter, sour, salty, hot, pungent, dry and burning. They may give momentary excitement but can cause health troubles in the long run. While some level of energy is essential, we must avoid excessive consumption of carbonated beverages and spicy snacks. These foods, if consumed in excess, can lead to energy crashes and disrupt sleep. Moderation is key when aligning with the concept of rajas or passion. It's important to balance the energizing aspects with a focus on overall health.
- **Tamasic Foods:** Tamasic foods are those that are stale, tasteless, bad-smelling, processed, or decomposed. Non-vegetarian food

is one example. These foods have a dulling effect on the mind. Overeating also falls into this category, leading to feeling sleepy and tired, resulting in potential health issues like obesity and indigestion. This aligns with the principle of tamas, or inertia, and we must be cautious of choices that can dull the body and mind.

- **Hygiene:** Avoid eating food from unclean places, as it can lead to health issues. Choose foods that are prepared in a clean and hygienic environment to ensure the safety and well-being of our body. It is best to eat homemade food as it is made in clean surroundings with better ingredients and love. It may seem simple at times but it's healthy and fulfilling. This aligns with the broader principle of maintaining cleanliness in our lives, contributing to overall health and vitality.
- **Gratitude:** Finally, cultivate a habit to be grateful before eating anything. It's only by God's grace that we are able to eat something. Thanking God before eating the food yourself makes the simple process of eating an opportunity to connect with God.

2. Balance in Sleeping

Adequate and quality sleep is foundational for physical and mental health.

- **Consistency:** Establish a consistent sleep schedule by going to bed and waking up at the same time every day, even on weekends. Aim for six to eight hours of sleep each night, as this allows the body to rest and rejuvenate. Ideally, try to go to bed within a couple of hours after sunset and wake up before sunrise. This way, your body remains healthy for long and your mind stays fresh and active.

  Regular physical exercises and breathing exercises help in achieving sound sleep.

  Avoid sleeping more than what your body requires. Oversleeping makes you lazy, dull and inactive.

  Avoid stimulants like caffeine close to bedtime. Create a

comfortable sleep environment and practise relaxation techniques to promote restful sleep.

- **Prayer:** Thank God before you sleep and offer prayers to Him as soon as you wake up. Incorporating prayers and meditation in your routine not only makes you stress free, but also invokes divine blessings. This helps you lead a more fulfilling life.

3. Balance in Work

Achieving balance in work involves effective time management and setting realistic goals. Break larger tasks into smaller, manageable chunks, and prioritize based on the importance of those tasks and their deadlines.

Avoid overcommitting and learn to say no when necessary. Take breaks during work to prevent mental fatigue and maintain productivity. Strive for a healthy work-life balance by establishing clear boundaries and allocating time for both academic/work responsibilities and personal life.

You don't need to be overly passionate to be productive. Real productivity springs from a balanced lifestyle, and not from an overly ambitious or restless work schedule.

4. Balance in Recreation

Recreation and leisure activities are vital for stress relief and mental well-being.

Schedule regular breaks during study or work sessions to prevent burnout. Engage in activities you enjoy, whether it's reading, listening to music, playing sports, spending time with friends or pursuing hobbies.

Recreation provides a mental reset, allowing you to return to tasks with renewed focus and creativity. It's important to strike a balance between productive work and enjoyable downtime.

Thus, balancing sleeping, eating, recreation, and work involves creating routines that prioritize self-care, setting realistic goals, and recognizing the importance of both productivity and relaxation. By paying attention to these aspects, you can enhance your overall health and well-being, leading to improved academic performance and a more enjoyable lifestyle.

Now that you have understood the power of balance and regulation, try to understand the power of meditation which helps you balance and regulate yourself. Learn more about it in the next chapter.

TRY THIS OUT!

Here is a table for you to fill and create the perfect balance in your life!

Activities	Are you balanced?	If yes, justify how. If no, explain how they can be balanced further.
Eating		
Sleeping		
Working		
Recreating		

3 The Magic of Mantra Meditation

One Mantra Changed His Life

Dhruva was a five-year-old prince. One day, his stepmother didn't allow him to sit on his father's lap. Dhruva's mind was filled with disappointment and anger. He left the palace and entered the forest alone. Along his journey, he met sage Narada. The sage asked, 'My dear boy, what are you doing alone in this wild forest?'

Dhruva replied, 'My stepmother insulted me. I want to take revenge on her. She didn't allow me to sit on my father's lap.'

Narada Muni said, 'You are a small child. Have a playful spirit and don't take honour and dishonour so seriously. I advise you to return home.'

'Dear sage, I want to worship Lord Vishnu and attain a position superior to even Lord Brahma. How can I prove myself?'

'Well, pleasing Lord Vishnu is not that easy. When you are grown up, you can come and worship the Lord and fulfil your desires.'

Dhruva didn't like to postpone his plans. He replied, 'Your advice is not penetrating my mind as I am very much affected by the insulting words of my stepmother. And my heart is longing to attain the greatest position in the world, one that no one has ever attained. Please tell me an honest means by which I can fulfil my desire.'

Narada Muni smiled, appreciating the child's determination. He then instructed, 'Dear Dhruva, please go to the banks of River Yamuna in the holy place of Vrindavan, and chant this mantra—*om namo bhagavata vaasudevaya.* The Lord will surely award what you desire.'

Dhruva then proceeded to Vrindavan and immersed himself in chanting the mantra, *om namo bhagavata vaasudevaya*, for six months, undeterred by distractions. His focused mantra meditation impressed Lord Vishnu who appeared in front of him to grant him a wish.

However, by chanting the mantra, Dhruva had achieved something more. Suddenly, he regretted holding revengeful feelings towards his stepmother. His heart was filled with forgiveness and kindness and there was no place for grudge and negativity. The mantra meditation purified his heart. In comparison to the Lord's omnipresence and benevolence, the great position he aspired for was insignificant. This positive transformation in his heart was due to his focused mantra meditation.

Takeaways from the Tale

- Mantra meditation has the potential to transform the heart and foster forgiveness.
- Mantra meditation is a great way to connect with the divine.
- Mantra meditation calms the mind agitated with negativity and distractions.
- Spiritual fulfilment often holds greater value than material aspirations.
- Seeking guidance from the wise and experienced contributes to a meaningful life journey.

What Is Mantra Meditation?

What Is Meditation?

In a general sense, *dhyana* or meditation refers to any form of deep thinking. For example, you may read a book and get lost in it, which can be called meditating on the book. But in a deeper sense, meditation refers to the process of evolving our mind from lower levels to higher levels, or inferior thoughts and desires to noble thoughts and desires. It's like climbing the stairs of a building to reach a higher floor where you can get a more pleasant view. The process may seem exhausting, but the end result is exciting.

What Is Mantra?

That word or statement which, by continuous repetition or recollection, protects us or yields several beneficial results is called a mantra (*mananāt trāyatē iti mantrah*). A mantra also protects our mind by regulating it (*manas trāyatē iti mantrah*). Several mantras mentioned in the scriptures are typically in the Sanskrit language and contain the names of the Supreme Divine.

What is Mantra Meditation?

It is the process of repeatedly focusing on one mantra for a long time. Of all types of meditation, mantra meditation is simplest and easiest. It is like reaching the higher floors in an elevator.

What is Japa?

When mantra meditation is done repeatedly by 'uttering' a spiritual mantra, it is called *japa*. When we only think of a mantra within our minds, we may sometimes get diverted to other thoughts. So great saints advised us to utter the mantra in a low voice so that we could hear it with our ears. Japa involves intently listening to the *mantra* we are uttering, while counting the number of times we are uttering it using beads for example. While the ears are attentively hearing, mouth is sincerely chanting and hands are carefully counting the mantras, the unnecessary thoughts in the mind subside, distractions are controlled and we make a connection with the divine.

Let us see some more benefits of mantra meditation.

Benefits of Mantra Meditation

Mantra meditation regulates and controls the mind. Repeatedly chanting a mantra is a traditional, spiritual and meditative practice. A sound, word, or a phrase when repeated, can have a calming, soothing and transformative effect on the mind. The idea is that the repetition of a mantra can serve as an effective tool for improving our concentration and ultimately benefit our spiritual well-being.

Develop a habit to chant a mantra for at least a few minutes in a day while trying to pull the mind back from all distractions. Just like a shield, these mantras, when chanted attentively, protect us from all sorts of distractions. Thus, it is one of the best ways to be the boss of our own minds! The following are a few benefits of chanting mantras daily.

- **Concentration Improvement:** Mantra meditation involves repetitive chanting, helping you focus your minds on a single sound vibration. This concentration practice can enhance your attention spans and improve your abilities to stay focused and mindful throughout the day. With increased levels of concentration and mindfulness, you can be more productive in your studies, extracurricular activities, and can make great spiritual advancement as well.

- **Emotional Regulation:** Regular mantra meditation assists you in managing your emotions. When you chant a divine name like Vasudeva, Krishna, Rama, Narayana, and so on, you develop a spiritual connection with the divine. The more you chant and meditate, the more you can maintain your calm even amidst chaotic circumstances. It also helps you develop emotional resilience and cope with stress.

- **Enhanced Memory:** The rhythmic repetition of mantras can stimulate the brain and improve memory retention. This can be beneficial for academic learning and focused study. You will be able to recollect book information and the teacher's lectures at the right time.
- **Promotes Mindfulness:** Mantra meditation encourages a state of mindfulness, where you become more aware of your thoughts and surroundings. This mindfulness can lead to greater self-awareness and emotional intelligence.
- **Stress Reduction:** The meditative nature of mantra chanting induces a sense of inner peace and relaxation, reducing your stress and anxiety levels.
- **Cultivates Positive Habits:** Introducing mantra meditation at a young age fosters positive habits related to mental well-being. It becomes a tool for self-care and emotional balance throughout your lives.

A Mantra to Calm Your Mind

There are unlimited mantras mentioned in the timeless scriptures. These mantras typically contain the names of the divine Lord, the Creator, Protector and Maintainer of all living beings. Mantras are an effective way to connect with the divine and invoke divinity within us.

Here is a simple mantra for chanting. This is called the *maha mantra* or the great mantra.

Hare Krishna Hare Krishna Krishna Krishna Hare Hare
Hare Rama Hare Rama Rama Rama Hare Hare

This mantra has only sixteen words, in which only three words are repeated. So, it's very easy to chant. When we say it with respect and love, it's like we're pushing the button on our magical elevator. Just like an elevator has a powerful force (electricity) that helps it go up quickly, the 'Hare Krishna maha mantra' has a magical power that lifts our thoughts and feelings up, up, up! It helps our thoughts go higher and higher, making us feel happy and light inside. It's like having a special key to unlock a door that leads to a place of joy and good thoughts.

We've just discovered the power of mantras! But are you curious to find out two new ways with which you can beat stress? Don't stress yourself thinking about what they could be! Just flip forward!

4 Breaks and Breathing Techniques

A Helping Hand

Emma was a hardworking student. One day, she immersed herself in a new project, working since early morning without any breaks.

It was 3 p.m. and she didn't even have any breakfast or lunch. Her mom had been asking her to eat but Emma didn't find time. Finally, her mom got her lunch plate and Emma started eating with a spoon while going through the project work. She finished her lunch within a few minutes and got back to working the same way.

Her brother saw her condition. She appeared tired and stressful. He came and said, 'Emma, let's go for a stroll.'

Emma replied, 'Not now, I need at least three more hours to complete my project.'

Her brother said, 'That's fine. Taking a little break will make you feel better. Come with me.' He then took her by hand into the garden and they both started walking.

He said, 'Sometimes, we get distracted every few minutes and sometimes, we work for hours without taking a break. Both are not good. Taking breaks at intervals and doing some breathing exercises can help you work more efficiently and feel less stressed. That way, you can manage your time well and stay focused without getting overwhelmed.'

They walked through the garden for a few minutes and sat under a tree. He then taught her a few breathing exercises. After a few minutes, Emma was back at her work. She felt more energetic and refreshed. She thanked her brother and continued her work.

Learning from this, Emma started taking short breaks during her study time. She also incorporated breathing exercises into her routine. This helped her work better and feel less stressed.

'Time Tracker'—Take Breaks

Taking breaks is like giving your brain a boost! Your brain needs a quick break to recharge and get ready for the next adventure. When you're working on your homework or a project, your brain works hard but it also needs some time to rest. Breaks help your brain stay focused and avoid feeling tired. They're like mini vacations in your daily routine. When you take a break, you're not giving up—you're actually making yourself stronger!

How to do:

Set a timer for your study sessions, say a thirty-minute slot. This is your 'concentration slot' where you firmly decide not to get up from your study or get distracted by anything. Even when your favourite show is on or a friend calls, you can't get up. When the timer rings, you promptly get up even if no one calls you. You take a short break of say five minutes to recharge and then dive back into your studies. It's like having your own study superhero clock guiding you through tasks!

You can set a timer to work for thirty, forty or even sixty minutes (whatever suits you best) and take five or ten-minute breaks after the timer goes off. But the principle is that continuous focus in a reasonable time frame, followed by a short break, facilitates our concentration and productivity.

Breaks keep you motivated and prevent you from feeling bored or overwhelmed.

What to do during breaks?

During your study or playtime, take a break, do a little dance, have a snack, or just do some stretching exercises. Your brain will thank you and you'll be ready for the next exciting task!

1. **Exercise:** Quick exercises during breaks refresh your mind and keep your energy levels up. Do jumping jacks or light stretching exercises during your breaks.
2. **Snacks:** Snacking on brain-boosting foods provides the energy your brain needs. Munch on nuts, fruits, or yogurt during your breaks. These snacks are like fuel for your brain, helping you stay sharp and focused. But mind you, don't overeat! That will make you lazy and sleepy and distract from your work.

3. **Walking:** Go for a stroll in your garden. Look at plants, flowers, sky and nature. But don't go too far as you will need to get back to your studies.
4. **Breathing:** Inhale slowly, hold it for a few counts, and then exhale. It's like your superhero breath that makes you ready for anything! Let's learn more about it now.

> **NOTE:** Don't pick up your phone during these breaks. It might seem that the phone will recharge you but actually, it just does the opposite!

Mindful Breathing

Your breath is like a magic wand that can make you feel calm and focused. Taking slow, deep breaths, is like preparing your brain for an exciting adventure with full enthusiasm. Mindful breathing exercises are like magic spells that can boost your concentration and reduce your stress.

Deep breaths are like a cozy hug for your nerves. They tell your body to relax and chill out, making it easier to concentrate on whatever task you're working on. Paying attention to your breath is like having a laser focus.

Let's learn some cool breathing techniques that can help beat stress the cool way!

Bee Breath (Bhramari)

Bhramari is a yogic breathing exercise also known as the 'bee breath' because it sounds like the buzzing of a bee. Here's how you can do it:

- **Find a Convenient Spot:** Sit in a comfortable position. You can sit on the floor or on a chair, whichever feels good for you.

- **Imagine You're a Bee:** Close your eyes and imagine you're a little bee, buzzing around happily.
- **Place your Hands:** Gently place your index fingers on your ears, your thumbs on your cheekbones and your other fingers on the sides of your nose.
- **Take a Deep Breath:** Inhale deeply through your nose. Feel your chest and belly fill up with air like a balloon.
- **Buzz like a Bee:** As you exhale, make a humming sound like a bee. Keep your mouth closed and make the sound deep within your throat.
- **Feel the Vibrations:** Feel the vibrations on your face and inside your head as you continue to hum.
- **Repeat:** Do this a few times, taking slow, deep breaths, enjoying the buzzing sounds all the while.

Why is the Bee Breath awesome for you?

- **Calms the Mind:** Bee Breath helps quieten your busy thoughts and makes your mind feel calm and peaceful.
- **Reduces Stress:** The humming sound is like a magic trick that helps make stress disappear.
- **Feels Fun:** Making the bee sound is lots of fun! It's like being a bee in your own imaginary garden.
- **Helps with Focus:** After doing the Bee Breath, you might feel more focused and ready for whatever comes next.

Lion Pose (Simhagarjana-asana)

'Simhagarjana asana' is also known as Lion Pose, and it's a fun yoga pose that imitates a lion's roar. Here's how you can do it:

- **Sit Comfortably:** Find a cozy spot to sit on your knees. You can use a soft mat or a cushion if you'd like.
- **Kneel Down:** Kneel down on your mat or the floor, making sure your knees are hip-width apart.
- **Place Your Hands:** Put your hands on your knees, like a friendly lion getting ready to play.
- **Roar Preparation:** Take a deep breath in through your nose. Imagine you're filling your belly with air.
- **Roar Out:** Open your mouth wide, stick out your tongue and roar loudly while exhaling. Imagine you're letting out a big lion roar!
- **Feel the Stretch:** While roaring and sticking your tongue out, stretch your face muscles and feel the stretch in your throat.
- **Repeat the Fun:** Do this a few times! Each time, see if you can make your lion roar even louder.

Why is the Lion Pose awesome for kids?

- **Fun and Playful:** It's like playing make-believe and being a roaring lion.
- **Relieves Tension:** Roaring in Lion Pose helps release any tension in your face and neck, making you feel more relaxed.
- **Express Yourself:** Lions express themselves by roaring, and in this pose, you get to release pent up emotions and express yourself too!

- **Boosts Confidence:** Making bold lion roars can make you feel strong and confident.

So, whenever you want to unleash your inner lion and have a bit of fun, give the Lion Pose a try!

Deep Belly Breathing

Deep belly breathing is a simple and fun way for us to relax. Here's how you can do it:

- **Find a Cozy Spot:** Sit comfortably on a chair or cushion. Make sure your back is straight.
- **Belly Balloon:** Place one hand on your chest and the other on your belly, like you're giving it a gentle hug.
- **Breathe In like a Balloon:** Inhale slowly through your nose. Feel your belly getting bigger, like you're inflating a balloon.
- **Breathe Out Slowly:** Exhale slowly. Imagine you're letting the air out of the balloon as your belly gets smaller.
- **Balloon Ride Game:** Pretend your belly is a balloon and you're giving it a happy ride. Inhale for the ride up and exhale for the ride down.

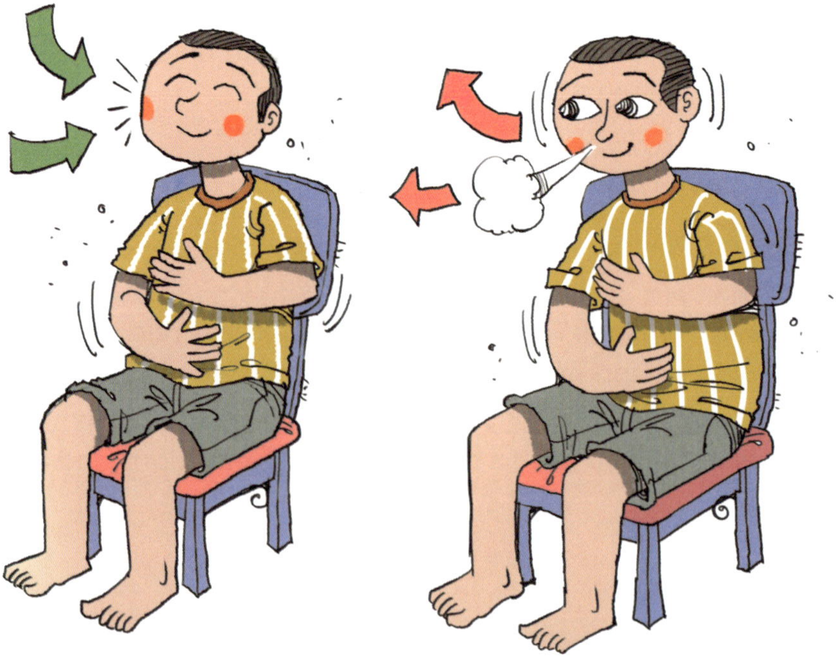

- **Count the Rides:** See how many rides your belly balloon can take. Each breath is like a joyful ride.
- **Feel the Calm:** Keep breathing in and out. Notice how your body feels calm and relaxed.

Why is Belly Breathing Awesome?

- **Stress Reduction:** It activates the body's relaxation response, reducing stress and promoting a sense of calm.
- **Improved Focus:** The mindful breathing process enhances concentration and helps clear the mind, leading to improved focus and mental clarity.
- **Balanced Energy:** Deep breathing balances the autonomic nervous system, promoting a balance between the sympathetic (fight-or-flight) and parasympathetic (rest-and-digest) systems.
- **Enhanced Mood:** The rhythmic nature of deep belly breathing can positively impact our mood, helping to alleviate feelings of anxiety and tension.
- **Better Sleep:** Incorporating deep breathing into our routine, especially before bedtime, can contribute to better sleep quality.

That's it! Deep belly breathing is like a little adventure for our belly, and it helps us feel peaceful and happy. Try it whenever you need a moment of relaxation!

CAUTION!

Breathing exercises done inappropriately can cause problems. So, perform these awesome exercises under the guidance of an elder or teacher.

5 Music, Prayers, and Chants

An Enlivening Beginning of the Day

A young Krish posed a curious question to his grandfather.
'Grandpa, when you were my age, how did you start your school day?'

Grandpa replied, 'Well, my school day would kick off with a prayer session. All students from different grades gathered in the common prayer hall to offer prayers to deities like Krishna, Rama, and Vishnu. We also praised the Goddess of learning, Sarasvati Devi, and sought blessings from Lord Ganesha, the remover of obstacles.'

Then, Krish asked, 'So, were these prayers all devotional?'

Grandpa explained, 'Not just devotional prayers. We also sang songs promoting unity, friendship, gratitude and love for humanity and the nation. It felt like a big family coming together, ready to start the day with smiles and positive vibes.'

This piqued Krish's interest. 'And what about when you started working?'

Grandpa reflected on the same. 'Well, my organization held important events, annual functions, and special gatherings with chants and prayers.'

Puzzled, Krish asked, 'What's the purpose of these prayers?'

Grandpa clarified, 'Prayers are a way to seek blessings from the divine and to dispel any negative forces, both external and internal.'

An amused Krish asked if his grandfather has continued this tradition.

'Yes, I continued to worship and pray at home, just like you see me doing every day. In many homes, people traditionally begin their day with prayers, meditation and spiritual chants to their preferred deities. It sets the tone for the day with a sprinkle of spiritual blessings.'

'Why are most of your prayers in Sanskrit, Grandpa?' asked Krish.

Grandpa answered, 'Prayer transcends language; it's about establishing a connection with the divine. While you can pray in any language, the divine philosophy and spiritual emotions of scriptures are beautifully conveyed in shlokas form our Vedas and Upanishads. Reading them directly provides a unique experience of their special power.'

Mulling over this, Krish asked, 'What's so special about a shloka?'

Grandpa explained, 'Like a small, zipped file in a computer reveals a large amount of data, a simple four-liner shloka contains wisdom in

a vast yet compact form when studied sincerely. Written by renowned sages, these shlokas are like a poetic formulae, offering solutions to life's various challenges.'

Impressed by this revelation, Krish asked, 'But aren't Sanskrit shlokas hard to remember?'

Grandpa reasoned, 'Consider this: is it easier to memorize a few prose statements or a few lines of poetry? Poetry, right? Similarly, the poetic Sanskrit shlokas are actually more enjoyable to remember than a paragraph of their translations. Learning them is like having an old yet effective key to open the treasure box of hidden wisdom.'

Inspired, Krish expressed his desire to include prayers in his daily routine and asked his grandpa to teach him some selected ones.

Power of Prayers

Prayers hold significant importance in various aspects of lives, contributing to our holistic development and well-being. Here are some key aspects highlighting the significance of prayers for us:

1. **Moral and Ethical Values:** Prayers often include teachings and values that promote morality, kindness, compassion and empathy. You can learn about the importance of honesty, integrity and treating others with respect.

2. **Spiritual Growth:** Engaging in prayers allows you to develop a sense of spirituality and connection to something larger than yourselves. It fosters a deeper understanding of their identity and purpose, encouraging a spiritual foundation for life.
3. **Emotional Well-being:** Praying can provide a sense of comfort and security. It offers a space for reflection, expression of emotions and seeking solace during challenging times. It can be a source of emotional support and resilience.
4. **Positive Habits and Discipline:** Praying daily instills discipline and a sense of structure in our lives. It helps us develop positive habits, including mindfulness, gratitude and a sense of responsibility.
5. **Cognitive Development:** Engaging in prayers often involves reciting verses, memorizing them and understanding their symbolic meanings. This contributes to cognitive development, memory retention and the ability to grasp abstract concepts.
6. **Building a Positive Outlook:** Prayers often focus on positive affirmations, gratitude and hope. Engaging in these practices can help us develop a positive outlook on life, fostering optimism and resilience in challenging times.
7. **Fostering a Sense of Purpose:** Through prayers, we are often reminded of our connection to a higher power and a greater purpose such as serving humanity. This sense of purpose can guide and motivate us as we navigate complexities of life.

Prayers offer a multifaceted approach to your development, encompassing moral, spiritual, emotional and cultural dimensions. They provide a foundation for character building, instill positive values, and contribute to overall well-being.

Soothing Music

Listening to soothing music on a daily basis can induce a sense of calmness in us. It reduces stress and anxiety levels and enhances our concentration levels. Spiritual music and chants not only calm our mind, but also invoke the blessings of the divine.

Spiritual music has a positive impact on our mood, masks distractions and creates a favourable environment for focused work. Additionally, it contributes to improved motivation and sustained attention.

Try this:

Create a personal playlist of calming tunes, soothing melodies, instrumental music, spiritual songs, mantra chanting, verse recitations, nature sounds, etc. Make a habit of listening to them regularly. You can also listen to some selected songs before you study.

Can you listen to music while studying?

Yes, you can. While preferences may vary for individuals, instrumental or ambient music is often recommended for studying or working, as it promotes learning without the potential distraction caused by the lyrics. Let it play softly in the background as you tackle your assignments. It's like having your personalized concentration soundtrack, making studying more enjoyable.

Music can significantly contribute to overall well-being in various ways:

- **Mood Regulation:** Music has the power to influence your moods. Upbeat and lively tunes can energize and uplift, while slower, calming melodies can help soothe and relax the mind. This contributes to emotional well-being.
- **Stress Reduction:** Listening to calming music has been shown to reduce stress levels. Music has the ability to soothe the mind and body, promoting relaxation and lowering the production of stress hormones.
- **Emotional Expression:** Music provides a powerful means to express and understand your emotions. Whether through listening or creating music, it allows you to explore a wide range of feelings, promoting emotional intelligence and self-awareness.

So, let's make it a fun habit of saying our prayers and listening to spiritual songs that make our hearts feel really good. Try it out and see how much joy it brings to your day!

TRY THIS OUT!

Incorporate the following prayers in your daily routine. Their meanings are also given for your understanding. It will take only a few minutes to recite these prayers.

oṁ saha nāvavatu saha nau bhunaktu
saha vīryaṁ karavāvahai
Tejasvi nāvadhītamastu mā vidviṣāvahai
Oṁ śāntiḥ śāntiḥ śāntiḥ

May we together be protected, may we together be nourished, may we work together with great energy. May our studies be enlightening and may we not have mutual hatred. May there be peace!

(Source: Yajurveda Taittiriya Upanishad)

oṁ pūrṇam adaḥ pūrṇam idaṁ
pūrṇāt pūrṇam udacyate
pūrṇasya pūrṇam ādāya
pūrṇam evāvaśiṣyate

The Supreme Lord is perfect and complete, and everything that emanates from Him, like this universe, is perfect and complete for the purpose it's meant for. Whatever is produced of the Complete Whole is also complete in itself. Because He is the Complete Whole, even though so many complete units emanate from Him, He remains the complete.

(Source: Isopanisad Invocation mantra)

tvameva mātā ca pitā tvameva,
tvameva bandhuśca sakhā tvameva
tvameva vidyā draviḍam tvameva,
tvameva sarvam mama deva deva

O Lord Sri Krishna, You are my mother and my father, You are my friend and my companion. You are knowledge and the Dravidian land. You are everything to me, O God of Gods.

(Source: Mahabharata)

paritrāṇāya sādhūnāṁ vināśāya ca dus-kṛtām,
dharma-saṁsthāpanārthāya sambhavāmi yuge yuge

Lord Krishna declared, 'For the protection of the righteous, for the destruction of the wicked, and for the establishment of righteousness, I come as an incarnation in every age.'

(Bhagavad Gita 4.8)

You can add many more beautiful verses to this list, but this is a short one for your daily practice and recitation. Try reciting these slokas daily and see how they empower you—mentally and spiritually.

In summary, spiritual music plays a multifaceted role in enhancing children's overall well-being by promoting emotional expression, reducing stress, supporting cognitive and social development and contributing to various aspects of one's physical, emotional, and social health.

TRY THIS OUT!

GRATITUDE JOURNAL

Try keeping a gratitude journal. Each day, write or draw something that you are thankful for. You could even compose a beautiful prayer of your own. Over a period of time, notice how such positive thinking reduces your stress.

6 Sharing Hearts and Seeking Help

Hope in a Hopeless Situation

The Ramayana is a wonderful story about Lord Rama and Mother Sita. When a mean demon king named Ravana took Sita away, Rama sent some *vanara* friends to find her. The strong and brave Hanuman, along with Jambavan, Nila, Angada, and other monkeys, headed south to look for Sita. Rama thought Hanuman was the best because he was strong, brave and clever.

Hanuman's group searched everywhere for Sita, but they couldn't find her even when they reached the ocean shore. Feeling disappointed, they decided to fast until death. Losing hope can be the biggest obstacle in life. The truly unfortunate are not those who face difficulties or lack resources, but those who have given up hope.

To uplift the spirits of the monkeys, a wise vulture named Sampati, who was Jatayu's brother, saw them. Sampati informed them that Sita was in Ravana's kingdom in Lanka, on the other side of the ocean. This news brought hope and joy to the monkeys, renewing their determination to find Mother Sita.

The monkeys felt another wave of disappointment when they saw the vast ocean. No one felt brave enough to jump across the hundred *yojanas*-wide ocean (one *yojana* was eight miles long). Witnessing the monkeys' sadness, Angada spoke up, suggesting that losing hope could be a cause for failure. He called upon those willing to leap a hundred yojanas to rescue Sita to come forward. Some monkeys could jump shorter distances, like ten, twenty, thirty, forty *yojana*s, and so on. Angada claimed he could jump a hundred *yojana*s, but he doubted if he could do it a second time on his return journey.

Jambavan said, 'Don't worry! We have mighty Hanuman. I consider him to be more than capable of completing our mission.' Jambavan continuously praised Hanuman, highlighting his extraordinary strength in various ways, igniting a powerful inspiration.

Encouraged and deeply moved by these words, Hanuman began to grow into an awe-inspiring, gigantic form.

To boost the spirits of the discouraged monkeys, Hanuman talked about his own achievements, saying, 'I can go around Mount Meru a thousand times without stopping. By splashing the ocean waters, I could flood the entire world. I can uproot the entire city of Lanka. I can find Mother Sita and bring happiness to Lord Rama's heart.'

All the monkeys were thrilled. Sometimes, to give much-needed reassurance to a disheartened person, a wise individual must speak confidently about their abilities, but without being falsely proud. This helps to impart hope and confidence.

Hanuman, filled with determination, offered prayers to his beloved Lord Rama and soared into the sky towards the golden city of Lanka on the other side of the ocean.

The Power of Positive Words

Genuine appreciation empowers and encourages a person, while fault-finding disempowers and weakens one's determination. Unnecessary fault-finding makes the faults true, even if they didn't exist before. Because of Jambavan's encouragement, Hanuman recalled his powers and got ready for his mission with confidence and courage.

Everyone glorifies Hanuman for crossing the ocean of Lanka, but it was Jambavan who inspired Hanuman to do so. Similarly, a well-wisher can identify the strengths in another and encourage them to grow to their fullest potential.

So, whenever you are confused or in a challenging situation that's beyond your ability to resolve, share your heart's conflicts with a trusted elder—your mother, father or

teacher. Seek their guidance and support. They will offer you the necessary motivation and direction to grow and glow.

Confusions are common. An arrogant person will try to solve all problems by one's own intelligence. But an intelligent person knows what to do in times of confusion—approach a teacher!

When the magnitude of your problem goes beyond the ability of your intelligence to solve, humbly approach a reliable guru for a solution. Such humility is real intelligence.

Takeaways from the Tale

- Hope is paramount; losing hope is the greatest impediment in life.
- A well-wishing elder identifies strengths, inspires, and empowers the young.
- Genuine appreciation empowers and inspires.

The Sweetness of Sharing Hearts

Sharing feelings with trusted elders builds a deep emotional connection and allows for the exchange of wisdom, values and experiences between different generations. Such intergenerational connections can forge positive effects on your well-being. Here are a few wonders of sharing your heart and seeking help from an elder:

1. **Wisdom and Experience Transfer:** Elders often possess a wealth of knowledge and life experiences. By sharing their stories, insights and life lessons, they contribute with valuable guidance by passing it on to the younger generation. This transfer of wisdom helps us navigate challenges which we haven't experienced before.

2. **Emotional Support:** Building strong emotional bonds between ourselves and elders can create a support system. We may find comfort, encouragement and a sense of security in the presence of caring and understanding elders. In turn, elders may experience joy and fulfilment in nurturing us and tapping into our new ways of thinking and performing tasks.
3. **Stress Reduction:** Because elders and well-wishers have a lot of knowledge and experience, they can inspire and motivate us to the best when we feel low. Thus, by lifting us up, they increase our happiness and reduce our stress quotient.

Children sharing their hearts with elders lies in the mutual exchange of wisdom, values, and emotional support. This intergenerational connection can contribute to the well-rounded development of both children and elders, helping them navigate life's challenges with a deeper understanding and a sense of shared purpose.

Respect elders and seek their blessings for a fulfilling childhood.

When you seek blessings, you purchase success at a discount.

Friends, siblings, parents, and teachers act as Jambavans in our lives and give us the necessary motivation, encouragement, and support. Thus, we can discover Hanuman within ourselves!

The Power of Affirmations

When you can't always get encouragement from others, affirmations can be of big help. An affirmation is like a special phrase or a string of positive words you say to yourself to feel good and motivated.

Remember, affirmations aren't about being overly confident or pretending to be a superhero. They're positive statements that help you become more determined and boost your confidence in a practical way. They can also help you concentrate better and become more mindful.

For example, you can say to yourself, 'I can do this,' or 'I'll be able to handle it,' or 'There is someone up there to support me.' These positive words act like power boosters, making you feel ready to face challenges.

Start your day by telling positive things to yourself. Even better, say a prayer to the Lord, who has all the power. It's like making a shield of positivity and confidence around you. You're already special and affirmations are here to remind you of the gifts you have from the Lord!

Stay awesome, stay focused and keep spreading those positive vibes!

TRY THIS OUT!

MORNING MAGIC: A 21-DAY CHALLENGE FOR A HAPPIER YOU!

Every morning, stand in front of the mirror and say, 'Dear Lord, you have lots of power and strength. Please give me the strength and bravery to handle tough situations. Help me see your support when things get tricky and let me do well in dealing with them or at least being unaffected by them.' Try saying this for twenty-one days and see how it makes a great difference in your life!

7 Being Self-resilient

The Itch and the Urge to Scratch

Arya was a clever boy. Recently he found a new special friend—his amazing smartphone filled with lots of fun games and apps. But Arya had a little problem; he couldn't stop spending time on it because the screen was just too captivating!

Arya would pick up his phone to check a quick message, but he would get lost in his phone for almost half an hour! When he realized he wasted so much time, he tried to focus on his work. But guess what? Throughout the day, the same thing kept happening, and Arya's playtime with his phone resulted in many unproductive hours. Arya desired to get back to his work, but he didn't have the determination to keep his phone aside.

One day, he expressed his difficulty to his caring mom. She gave him some helpful advice. 'Make a promise to yourself that you'll not spend more than thirty to sixty minutes a day with your phone. Keep track of the time you are spending on it.'

Arya really wanted to follow his mom's advice, but he found it hard to resist the fun of his digital friend. One day, things took a different turn. Arya felt an itchy sensation in his hand and started scratching it for relief. The moment he stopped scratching, he found the itching sensation increasing. It turned into a big problem! The itchiness spread to other parts of his body and Arya couldn't stop scratching until his skin became all red and puffy.

Arya, feeling really uncomfortable, went to his mom for help. She took him to a doctor who gave him a tablet and a tiny injection to stop the itchiness. The doctor also told Arya to use some special ointment.

The doctor advised Arya, saying, 'Don't scratch anymore. If you scratch on the infected part with your nails even once, you will feel like scratching more. The more you scratch, the more the infection would increase and spread to other parts of the body. You may even bleed. Scratching seems to give you immediate relief, but it is not the solution. It is only a means to aggravate the problem.'

Arya understood that if he controls his urge to scratch the infected hand, he could save himself from a lot of trouble. He went home with his mom and started the medication.

At home, Arya's mom made a sound analogy and shared it with him. 'Arya, just like how scratching led to spreading of the itchiness, distractions can spread in your mind. Just like scratching once made you feel like scratching more and more, checking the phone once will make you feel like exploring it more and more. The solution is to control that first urge.'

Arya understood the parallels between his digital distraction and itching sensation. His mom concluded with her original advice, 'Take a firm affirmation that you would use the phone only when absolutely necessary. Follow it with determination. This way, you won't lose precious time and can focus on what truly matters. We can't always get support from others. Elders can tell you what is right and what is wrong. But it's your responsibility to follow the right thing and avoid the wrong ones. That requires determination.'

Arya took two

affirmations—'I wouldn't use the smartphone for more than an hour each day,' and 'I wouldn't scratch my infected hand.' He was determined to control digital distractions and to resist the urge to scratch. Gradually, his days became more focused and he discovered the joy of being present in the moment.

Takeaways from the Tale

- Set personal limits on smartphone usage for increased focus and productivity.
- Recognize that distractions, like itching, can spread in your mind; minimize them for better concentration.
- Seek help early when facing challenges, as prompt action can prevent problems from worsening.
- Embrace the joy of being present in the moment by controlling distractions and resisting technological temptations.

Tolerate to Grow in Life

As we become wiser and understand what's not good for us, it's important to learn to say no to harmful things. In the Gita, Lord Krishna advises us not to be swayed by temporary pleasures and to choose what we need the most over what feels good in the moment. He explained that those who endure temporary distractions are the happiest in the long run.

Much like Arya, who learned to stay determined and resist the urge to pick up the phone for the sake of studies, we should also practice tolerating temptations. These distractions might offer a brief moment of happiness, but they can prevent us from experiencing longer-lasting joy.

Constant distractions can bump up our stress levels. In our adventure of growing wiser, saying no to tricky distractions is like discovering the secret map to lasting joy. Just like Arya's bravery to resist phone temptations for his studies, being strong against tricky situations is super cool! Remember, choosing lasting happiness over quick pleasures is the magic tool for a balanced life!

TRY THIS OUT!

FREEZE YOUR TEMPTATIONS

Identify five temptations that you simply can't resist. It could be your smartphone, a cheesecake or even your favourite comic. Now place them on your study desk creating a temptation zone. As you look at each one of them, pretend to freeze and think how you can overcome the allure that the specific item casts on you. Note your thoughts and apply your ideas to see your tolerance grow!

Acknowledgements

Words fall short of expressing my gratitude to Srila Prabhupada, the founder Acharya of the International Society for Krishna Consciousness (ISKON), who presented the magnum opus literature Bhagavad Gita with his lucid explanations. It is through the lens of his illuminating purports that I have learnt to understand the depth of the Gita.

I am forever indebted to my beloved guru, His Holiness Radhanath Swami, the founder of Govardhan Ecovillage and an international bestselling author, for enlightening me on the ideal mood of scriptural study and encouraging me with his kind blessings. I learnt profound truths of life by hearing his discourses and observing his exemplary dealings. I express my earnest gratitude to my mentor Gauranga Prabhu and many other great spiritual teachers and friends who inspired me in various ways in my spiritual journey.

I can't thank Tanay Shah enough for his enthusiastic inputs and patiently editing the manuscript. I am grateful to Parth Shah for his wonderful editing and encouraging suggestions. With the honest and selfless efforts of these two young friends, this book took such a beautiful shape.

I am sincerely grateful to Sakshi Sharma for meticulously editing the manuscript and her efficient coordination in the publication of this book. My heartfelt thanks also go to Charbak Dipta for providing captivating illustrations that enhance the easy assimilation of the book's contents for children. I extend my appreciation to the entire team at Scholastic India for making this publication possible, benefiting children across the globe. I sincerely thank Sagar Wadekar and Mansi Wadekar for their wonderful support and coordination.

Finally, I heartily thank all the wonderful children who attended my multiple online and onsite classes and courses and gave me an understanding of their thoughts and needs through their innocent and intelligent questions. I congratulate their parents and teachers who trained them so well. It's my great pleasure to offer one more gift to them in the form of this book.

About the Author

Gauranga Darshan Das, a disciple of Radhanath Swami, is a distinguished educator. He holds a master's degree in Systems Science and Automation from the prestigious Indian Institute of Science (IISc), Bengaluru, India. During his brief corporate career, spanning approximately two years, he conducted research at esteemed organizations such as TCS Innovation Labs, resulting in the publication of over ten technical papers and the filing of a provisional patent. His unique journey also led him to embrace the path of monkhood in 2009.

In his current role as the Dean of Bhaktivedanta Vidyapitha at ISKCON Govardhan Ecovillage (GEV), outside Mumbai, Gauranga Darshan Das conducts spiritual education programmes in both residential and online platforms. He is a prolific speaker and teacher, renowned for presenting timeless wisdom in a lucid and contemporary form to various audiences, including children, teens, professionals and educators. He travels to various places in India, Australia, United States, etc., to share wisdom in various forums including temples, ashrams, schools, colleges and the corporate sector. He has lectured for over 7500 hours and conducted over fifty online courses (www.vidyapitha.in).

As an accomplished author, he has penned more than thirty-five books. He runs a monthly e-zine called the *Bhagavata Pradipika* and regularly contributes to national as well as international publications, including the *Back to Godhead* magazine. His dedication to the dissemination of spiritual wisdom has made him a respected figure in spiritual, educational and corporate circles.

Know more about him on **www.gaurangadarshan.com**